BR DIESEL LOCOMOTIVES IN PRESERVATION

BR DIESEL LOCOMOTIVES IN PRESERVATION

Fred Kerr

PEN & SWORD
TRANSPORT

First published in Great Britain in 2018 by
Pen & Sword Transport
An imprint of
Pen & Sword Books Ltd
47 Church Street
Barnsley
South Yorkshire
S70 2AS

ISBN 978 1 52671 308 7

Typeset in 11pt Minion by Mac Style Ltd, Bridlington, East Yorkshire
Printed and bound in India by Replika Press Pvt Ltd

Pen & Sword Books Limited incorporates the imprints of Atlas, Archaeology, Aviation, Discovery, Family History,
Fiction, History, Maritime, Military, Military Classics, Politics, Select, Transport, True Crime, Air World,
Frontline Publishing, Leo Cooper, Remember When, Seaforth Publishing, The Praetorian Press,
Wharncliffe Local History, Wharncliffe Transport, Wharncliffe True Crime and White Owl.

For a complete list of Pen & Sword titles please contact
PEN & SWORD BOOKS LIMITED
47 Church Street, Barnsley, South Yorkshire, S70 2AS, England
E-mail: enquiries@pen-and-sword.co.uk
Website: www.pen-and-sword.co.uk

Front Cover: A yard view at Barrow Hill (BHR) on 7 October 2001 during the autumn diesel gala when Class 17 D8568 was a 'guest' locomotive; Class 55 '*Deltic*' D9009 *Alycidon* was heading the shuttle service and Class 85/1 85101 was stabled in the yard as a display item.

Rear Cover: A dreich day at Oxenhope on 15 June 2007 during the Keighley & Worth Valley Railway's (KWVR) 2007 diesel gala sees Class 20 visitor D8020 + resident 20031 depart with the 12:45 Oxenhope–Keighley service whilst Class 25/1 25059 waits in the carriage siding for its next duty.

Contents

Section 1: Shunting Locomotives 8

1.1: Pre-Nationalization Designs 8

1.2: Post-Nationalization Designs 11

Section 2: Main Line Locomotives 32

2.1: Type 1 Designs 34

2.2: Type 2 Designs 41

2.3: Type 3 Designs 62

2.4: Type 4 Designs 80

2.5: Type 5 Designs 108

Section 3: Heritage Centres 115

3.1: Barrow Hill Roundhouse (BHR) 115

3.2: Bo'ness & Kinneil Railway (BKR) 117

3.3: Embsay & Bolton Abbey Railway (EBAR) 118

3.4: East Lancashire Railway (ELR) 120

3.5: Great Central Railway (GCR) 121

3.6: Keighley & Worth Valley Railway (KWVR) 122

3.7: Severn Valley Railway (SVR) 124

A collection of nose-fronts at Barrow Hill (BHR) seen on 12 August 2006 during a diesel gala reveals (from left to right) Class 20; Class 47; Class 37 and Class 20 examples.

When British Railways (BR) introduced its Modernisation Plan in 1954 to herald the replacement of steam traction by a fleet of modern diesel and electric powered traction, it recognised that it only had experience of operating six main line diesel locomotives. That experience, however, had identified that the new traction comprised three elements, namely (1) engine (prime mover) to provide power (2) transmission to transmit power to the driving wheels and (3) body (mechanical portion) to contain the other 2 portions. This led to the creation of a Pilot Scheme to trial the various combinations of these three elements and for which 174 locomotives were ordered in November 1955.

The scheme began well but political pressure and changes in government policies throughout the next decade saw the initial Pilot Scheme replaced by bulk orders for Pilot Scheme designs from early 1957 and it was only in August 1968, when steam traction was officially eliminated, that BR was finally able to review the situation with a National Traction Plan. This took note of the post-Beeching environment of increasing competition from road transport whilst identifying locomotive designs which had proved to be unsuccessful or were thought unsuitable for future use operating on the 'modern' railway.

At this time the nascent heritage movement was concentrating on the preservation of steam locomotives, hence the interest in diesel traction was restricted to shunting locomotives, and it was only in 1977, with the preservation of Class 42 'Warship' D821 *Greyhound* (funded privately by the nascent Diesel Traction Group) and the Class 35 'Hymek' D7017 (funded by public subscription), that main line diesel locomotives began to be purchased for preservation. Whilst most purchases were simply for use on heritage lines, some locomotives were bought with the buyers' aspiration of being able to operate on the main line once more.

Once bought, owners faced the task of restoring their purchases to working order and, once successful, show them off at heritage lines. By the early 1980s many proposed heritage lines found that the pool of available steam locomotives had been exhausted and realised that diesel locomotives were the only source of traction available. This saw them offering facilities for the restoration and operation of diesel locomotives, leading to some lines being recognised as being 'diesel-friendly' whilst others were totally against mixing steam traction and main line diesel traction. The parallel development of owners being more willing to transfer their locomotives between heritage lines led to some lines, such as the Bo'ness & Kinneil Railway, the East Lancashire Railway, the Keighley & Worth Valley Railway and the Severn Valley Railway, becoming as well known for their operation of diesel traction, with their associated galas, as for their operation of steam traction.

This album seeks to pay tribute to those early diesel preservation pioneers by showing the variety of diesel locomotives that have been successfully preserved by enthusiasts. Some have been returned to working order whilst some rarer examples are still undergoing lengthy restoration due to the difficulty of sourcing necessary parts, but all are supported by willing volunteers who both appreciate and value their charges. Their combined efforts now serve to illustrate both the development and history of diesel locomotives since their initial introduction by BR under its Modernisation Plan and gratitude is due to the heritage lines which understand that diesel traction is as much part of the history of Britain's railways that they seek to preserve as steam traction.

Fred Kerr
October 2017

Section 1:
Shunting Locomotives

1.1: Pre-Nationalization Designs

Whilst many steam locomotive manufacturers had begun the development of small diesel shunting locomotives after their success in the First World War, the main line railway companies remained committed to steam locomotives with most locomotives being built within their own workshops. One major exception was the London Midland Scottish Railway Company (LMSR) which by the late 1920s had identified steam locomotive shunters as an expense which needed to be reduced and began trialling locomotives from outside builders during the 1930s as it sought to identify standard designs for its future needs.

Turning to established builders the LMSR bought small shunters (100–250 hp) from the Hunslet Engine Company Ltd and large shunters (300–400 hp) from both Armstrong Whitworth and English Electric for comparison.

1.1.1: Hunslet Engine Co Ltd

Builder
Hunslet Engine Co

Year Built
1933

Engine
MAN 6-Cylinder 150 hp @ 900 rpm

Transmission
Mechanical

LMSR Fleet Numbers
7401–7404 (later 7051–7054)

Ordered as one of four locomotives with different combinations of engine and transmission, 7401 was operated from Leeds Hunslet Road adjacent to its builder's workshops. It was renumbered 7051 by the LMSR in 1934 and by 1936 was based at Chester. At the onset of the Second World War the four locomotives were borrowed by the War Department (WD) with 7051 being returned to, and borrowed from, the LMSR during 1940–45. On return to the LMSR in 1945, 7051 was sold to Hunslet in December 1945. The locomotive was fitted with a McLaren Ricardo MR6 diesel engine rated at 132 hp and used for short-term hire until being sold to the Middleton Railway Trust in 1960, where it was named *John Alcock*.

7051 is in LMS guise as it works a shuttle service on the demonstration line at Barrow Hill (BHR) during a diesel gala on 5 October 2003.

1.1.2: *London Midland Scottish Railway Company*

Builder
LMSR/BR Derby; BR Darlington

Year Built
1945–1952

Engine
English Electric 6-cylinder 6KT rated at 350 hp @ 680 rpm

Transmission
Electric

Fleet Numbers
LMSR = 7100–7109; 7120–7155; BR = 12033–12138

History: The LMSR was interested in a large shunter for use in busy yards and light inter-yard trip working and trialled two designs in 1935 – placing orders with Armstrong Whitworth (AW) (LMSR Nos. 7059–7068) using a Sulzer engine and jackshaft electrical transmission and Hawthorn Leslie (HL) (LMSR Nos. 7069–7078) using an English Electric engine and electric transmission linked directly to a traction motor on each outer axle.

The result of the trials was to identify the AW locomotives layout as superior but the company had ceased locomotive production in 1937 to concentrate on armaments production, hence the LMSR elected to build further locomotives at its Derby works.

It initially built thirty locomotives (LMSR Nos. 7080–7099 and 7110–7119) to the AW layout, albeit with English Electric 6KT engines, but subsequently adopted the HL drive train (LMSR Nos. 7100–7109) for the War Department in 1940 and this became the standard configuration for future designs.

Further orders to the 'standard' design appeared in the 1940s with orders for LMSR 7120–32 (later BR 12033–45) and Ministry of Supply 70260–70273; after the Second World War the LMSR continued building the class and this continued after the 1948 nationalization with Derby finalising building at 12102 whilst a batch of locomotives (12103–12138) was delivered from Darlington Works for the Eastern Region (ER) of BR between March 1952 and January 1953.

AD601 was the 13th locomotive built as part of the order for twenty supplied to the Ministry of Supply in 1945 and was delivered to Longmoor Military Railway (LMR). It was subsequently renumbered to 878 in 1952 and finally to AD601 in 1980 prior to being sold to the Lakeside & Haverthwaite Railway (LHR) in December 1980. On the LHR it sometimes (confusingly) carries LMSR guise as 7120 although the original LMSR 7120 was renumbered to 12033 by BR and withdrawn from service in January 1969.

AD601 approaches Newby Bridge (LHR) on 6 March 2015 whilst working the Lakeside–Haverthwaite leg of a railway tour chartered by the Preserved Locomotives Enthusiasts Group (PLEG).

12077 entered service at Saltley depot in October 1950 and was withdrawn from Wigan Springs Branch depot in October 1971. It was sold into industrial service in 1972 from where it entered preservation with the Midland Railway Centre (MRC) at Butterley in February 1979.

Left: 12077 acts as shed pilot on 8 November 2014 whilst shunting Standard Class 5 4-6-0 73129 into the shed building at Swanwick Junction (MRC).

12099 entered service at Nottingham depot in February 1952 and was withdrawn from Bletchley depot in July 1971. It was sold into industrial service in March 1972 from where it entered preservation with the Severn Valley Railway (SVR) in March 1990.

Below: 12099 is paired with Class 08 D3201 as they approach Kidderminster (SVR) on 2 October 2015 whilst hauling the 10:10 Bewdley–Kidderminster service during the annual diesel gala event.

1.2: Post-Nationalization Designs

When the UK railway companies were formed into British Railways (BR) from 1 January 1948, the LMSR became the London Midland Region (LMR) and continued building its 0-6-0 diesel design. That design however was found to be too heavy for smaller yards such as industrial sidings and docksides hence the nascent BR turned to industry for smaller 0-4-0 and 0-6-0 designs with power ranges from 150 hp to 250 hp.

This demand was met by such builders as Andrew Barclay (D2400–2409; D2410–2444; D2953–2956); Drewry Car (D2200–2214; D2215–2273; D2274–2341); Hudswell Clarke (D2500–2519; D2550–2618); Hunslet Engine Co (D2950–2952); North British Locomotive Co (D2700–2707; D2708–2780; D2900–2913); Ruston & Hornsby (PWM651–654; D2957–2958; D2985–2998) and Yorkshire Engine Co (D2850–2869) whilst BR's workshops at Swindon and Doncaster shared the production of D2000–2199; D2372–2399.

1.2.1: Pre-TOPS Designs

BR introduced its TOPS (Total Operations Processing System) in the late 1960s and extended it to cover its locomotive fleet in the early 1970s by which time the changed operating environment of the railways had led to the withdrawal of many diesel shunting locomotives. Whilst some were sold to larger industrial concerns, the growing interest in preserving steam traction saw many locomotives being scrapped and it was mainly those examples sold to industry which were fortunate to enter preservation once the nascent heritage lines appreciated their value for both maintenance tasks and standby passenger duty.

1.2.1.1: Hudswell Clarke & Company

Builder
Hudswell Clarke & Co

Year Built
1961

Engine
Gardner 8L3 rated at 204 hp @ 1200 rpm

Transmission
Mechanical

BR Fleet Numbers
D2510–2519

D2511 stands in Oxenhope sidings (KWVR) on 10 October 2015 where it is based for stock shunting duties in the carriage sidings and workshops.

D2511 entered service at Barrow depot in August 1961 and remained there until withdrawn in December 1967. It was sold to industry from where it entered preservation with the Keighley & Worth Valley Railway (KWVR) in August 1977.

1.2.1.2: North British Locomotive Company

Builder
North British Locomotive Co

Year Built
1957–1961

Engine
North British M.A.N. W6V rated at 225 hp @ 1100 rpm

Transmission
Hydraulic

BR Fleet Numbers
11708–719 (later D2708–2719); D2720–2780

D2767 entered service at Eastfield Depot in August 1960 from where it was withdrawn in June 1967 and sold into industry. It entered preservation with the Bury Transport Museum, associated with the nascent East Lancashire Railway (ELR), in 1981 and was subsequently sold to the Scottish Railway Preservation Society (SRPS) at Bo'ness where it is based as at July 2016.

1.2.1.3: Ruston & Hornsby

Builder
Ruston & Hornsby

Year Built
1963 [650]; 1959 [651–654]

Engine
Ruston & Hornsby 6-cylinder 6VPH rated at 165 hp @ 1250 rpm

Transmission
Electric

BR Fleet Numbers
PWM650–654; TOPS = 97650–654

PWM651 entered service as Western Region Departmental stock, numbered Permanent Way Machine (PWM) 651, at Cardiff in August 1959 where it worked until withdrawal in October 1998; in 1979 it was renumbered into the Departmental Class 97 series to become 97651. It initially entered preservation with the Swindon & Cricklade Railway (SCR) but was subsequently sold to the Northampton & Lamport Railway (NLR) then to the Strathspey Railway (SR) where it is resident as at December 2016.

Left: D2767 is displayed as an exhibit in the SRPS Scottish Railway Museum at Bo'ness on 24 August 2009 whilst awaiting its turn for overhaul.

Right: 97651 lies stored in the sidings at Chapel Brampton on 13 August 2005 during its sojourn on the NLR.

Builder
English Electric

Year Built
1957

Engine
English Electric 6RKT rated at 500 hp @ 750 rpm

Transmission
Electric

BR Fleet Numbers
D0226–7

1.2.1.4: English Electric Demonstrator

D0226 was one of two prototype shunting locomotives produced by English Electric; supplied with a 500 hp engine, D0226 had an electric transmission whilst D0227 had a hydraulic transmission in order to provide comparison between the two transmission systems. Both locomotives were intended for shunting and trip working duties but in service they were found too powerful for shunting duties and not powerful enough for trip workings.

D0226 entered service at Stratford depot along with D0227 in July 1957 from where they were withdrawn and returned to English Electric in October 1960. D0226 remained in store until March 1966 when it entered preservation with the Keighley & Worth Valley Railway (KWVR) on 'long term loan'. On the KWVR it has proved a valued locomotive capable of working both service trains and the numerous infrastructure services required by the maintenance teams.

D0226 Vulcan powers a maintenance train in Oakworth yard (KWVR) on 16 August 2014.

1.2.2: TOPS Designs

Despite the cull of small shunting locomotives whilst BR contracted during the 1960s, the application of the TOPS system in the 1970s was still able to identify thirteen classes which operated on BR's network. The withdrawal of these locomotives still continued with many being sold to industry but enthusiasts were beginning to appreciate both the history and value of them hence the increase in the number of locomotives which entered preservation. Some examples were bought directly from BR itself or from industrial concerns once their working lives had come to an end but all were bought as appreciation of their value to heritage lines became increasingly clear.

NOTE: The classes in this and following sections are detailed in numerical order of TOPS classification rather than by date of introduction or numerical order of BR fleet number.

1.2.2.1: Class 01 – Andrew Barclay and Sons

Builder
Andrew Barclay & Sons

Year Built
1956

Engine
Gardner 6L3 rated at 153 hp @ 1200 rpm

Transmission
Mechanical

BR Fleet Numbers
11503–6 (later D2953–6); TOPS = 01.001–2

D2956 takes a break from shed pilot duties on 20 May 2006 as it rests in Castlecroft yard (ELR) adjacent to the ELR's Bury–Rawtenstall line.

D2956 entered service as 11506 at Stratford depot in March 1956 and was withdrawn from Doncaster depot in January 1966 whence it was sold to industry. It was used by Mayer-Newman scrap merchants until withdrawn from service in 1984 with a defective transmission. It was subsequently donated by the company to the East Lancashire Railway (ELR), arriving in Bury during 1985.

The history of this locomotive has been confused by the actions of BR who, when D2956 was withdrawn, allocated the fleet number to Departmental locomotive 81 which was a similar locomotive in appearance. The latter locomotive was also sold to industry on withdrawal from BR service but was cut up at the end of its industrial service, although confusion still arises as the original D2956 also carries the works plate of AB 397 instead of its actual AB 398 works plate.

1.2.2.2: Class 02 – Yorkshire Engine Company

Builder
Yorkshire Engine Co

Year Built
1960–61

Engine
Rolls Royce C6NFL rated at 179 hp @ 1800 rpm

Transmission
Hydraulic

BR Fleet Numbers
D2850–2869; TOPS = 02.001–004

History: This class of locomotive was ordered to replace the L&YR Class 19 0-4-0ST locomotives used on Merseyside dock lines.

D2860 entered service at Fleetwood depot in September 1961 and was withdrawn from Allerton Depot in December 1970. It remained in store until entering preservation with the National Rail Museum (NRM) at York where it is often used as 'shed pilot' for stock moves around the NRM site.

Above: On 22 June 2010 D2860 shunted A1 Class 4-6-2 60163 Tornado into the Display Yard whilst …

Below: … on 29 February 2016 it shunted A3 Class 4-6-2 60103 Flying Scotsman into the Display Yard prior to the start of a photography charter organised by the NRM.

1.2.2.3: Class 03 – British Railways

Builder
BR Doncaster; BR Swindon

Year Built
1957–1961

Engine
Gardner 8L3 rated at 204 hp @ 1200 rpm

Transmission
Mechanical

BR Fleet Numbers
11187–11211 (later D2000–2024); D2025–2199; D2370–2399; TOPS = 03.001–399

History: In the early days of BR the supply of small shunting locomotives was obtained from private industry but in 1957 BR decided to produce its own design based on the Drewry prototype that had been supplied in June 1947, and subsequently taken into Southern Region Departmental stock as DS1173 in 1948. The initial order for forty-three locomotives was placed with Swindon Works with subsequent orders being shared between Swindon and Doncaster Works.

D2148 entered service at York depot in June 1960 and was withdrawn from Healey Mills depot in November 1971 whence it was sold into industrial service. It entered preservation with Southport's Steamport Museum in March 1987 and moved with that operator's transfer to the Ribble Steam Railway (RSR) in Preston during 1999.

D2148 forms the rear of a Strand Road–Riversway shuttle service as it crosses the Marina Bridge (RSR) on 3 October 2015.

D2072 entered service at Bradford (Hammerton St) depot in October 1959 and was withdrawn from Darlington depot in March 1981 to enter preservation with the Lakeside & Haverthwaite Railway (LHR).

Left: **D2072 carries TOPS number 03072 on 6 March 2015 as it passes Newby Bridge (LHR) with the Haverthwaite–Lakeside leg of a tour of the line chartered by the Preserved Locomotives Enthusiast Group (PLEG).**

D2117 entered traffic at Swansea Danycraig depot in September 1959 and was withdrawn from Wigan Springs Branch depot in October 1971 whence it entered preservation with the Lakeside & Haverthwaite Railway (LHR) shortly after.

Below Left: **Operating as 03066 in BR's corporate blue livery, D2066 draws Ivatt Class 4MT 2-6-0 43106 onto the turntable at Barrow Hill on 23 September 2015 during a steam gala event.**

D2066 entered service at York depot in August 1959 and was withdrawn from Gateshead depot in January 1988 whence it was sold into industrial service. It subsequently entered preservation with the Barrow Hill Roundhouse (BHR) where it sees regular use as shed pilot.

Below Right: **Partnered by sister locomotive D2072 in black livery, D2117 stands in Haverthwaite yard on 16 November 2008 prior to working a Haverthwaite–Lakeside service during a rare Diesel Day on the LHR.**

1.2.2.4: *Class 04 – Drewry Car Company*

Builder
Vulcan Foundry; RSH Newcastle; RSH Darlington

Year Built
1952–1962

Engine
Gardner 8L3 rated at 204 hp @ 1200 rpm

Transmission
Mechanical

BR Fleet Numbers
11100–11115 (later D2200–2214); 11121–11135 (later D2215–2229); 11149–11160 (later D2230–2241); 11212–11249 (later D2242–2259); D2260–2340; D2341; TOPS = Class 04 (TOPS numbers never carried)

History: This class originated with the demonstrator locomotive supplied to the London North Eastern Railway Company in 1947 and which the company tested but rejected because it was looking to design its own shunting locomotive. With the formation of BR shortly after in 1948, the locomotive was trialled with the Southern Region where it was purchased and transferred to Departmental stock to become DS1173. In March 1967 the locomotive was returned to operating stock based at Hither Green depot where it was renumbered to D2341 and worked until withdrawn from Ashford depot in December 1968.

D2203 entered service at March depot in June 1952 and was withdrawn from Crewe Works in December 1967 whence it was sold into industrial service. It entered preservation with the Yorkshire Dales Railway (YDR) – later Embsay & Bolton Abbey Railway (EBAR) – where it acts as the line's 'rescue' locomotive as at December 2016.

D2203 shunts coach bogies at Embsay station (EBAR) on 27 September 2015.

D2302 entered service at Lincoln depot in October 1960 and was withdrawn from Derby depot in June 1969 whence it was sold into industrial service. It entered preservation in September 1993 with the South Yorkshire Railway (SYR) as part of the Harry Needles (HNRC) collection; it was sold to the D2578 Group in November 2011 and transferred to a new base at Moreton Park (by Hereford).

Left: D2302 stands in the store line at HNRC's base at Barrow Hill Roundhouse on 15 July 2007.

Right: D2203 awaits departure from Bolton Abbey (EBAR) on 29 October 2006 with the 12:30 service to Embsay formed of 3-car Class 107 trainset 52005+59791+52031.

D2246 entered traffic at Hull depot in December 1956 and was withdrawn from Knottingley depot in July 1968 whence it entered industrial service. It subsequently became part of the HNRC collection in 1994 from where it was sold to enter preservation with the South Devon Railway (SDR) in January 2001.

Left: D2246 stands in the yard at Buckfastleigh on 20 July 2005 – the base of the SDR.

1.2.2.5: *Class 05 – Hunslet Engine Company*

Builder
Hunslet Engine Company

Year Built
1955–1961

Engine
Gardner 8L3 rated at 204 hp @ 1200 rpm

Transmission
Mechanical

BR Fleet Numbers
11136–11176 (later D2550–2573); D2574–2618; TOPS = 05.001

D2595 entered service at York depot in January 1960 and was withdrawn from Thornton Junction depot in June 1968 whence it was sent to its builder (Hunslet Engine Company) for scrapping. After a lengthy period in store it was sold into industry in 1969 from where it was sold into preservation with the East Lancashire Railway (ELR). It was subsequently sold to a member of Steamport and transferred to the Southport site in 1989 then subsequently to the Ribble Steam Railway (RSR) site in 1999.

Right: **D2595 crosses the Marina Bridge (RSR) on 7 March 2015 whilst working a shuttle service from Riverview–Strand Rd.**

D2554 entered service as 11140 at Parkeston Quay depot in May 1956 and was transferred to Ryde depot (Isle of Wight) on 7 June 1966. It was transferred to Departmental stock in February 1981 and renumbered to 97803. It entered preservation with the neighbouring Isle of Wight Steam Railway (IoWSR) on 23 August 1984.

Below: **Now restored to Green livery, D2554 was a display item at the Haven St base of the IoWSR on 12 March 2011.**

D2595 is a stalwart of the RSR fleet with scenes from the line including:

Right: Standing in the 'new' facility yard on 11 January 2004 in BR green livery.

Below Left: Standing at the head of a trainset of bitumen tanks, associated with the Ribble Rail contract with Lindsey Oil Refinery, at Riversway station on 7 March 2015 whilst awaiting its next duty during a gala event.

Below Right: Entering the RSR 'estate' on 23 February 2011 whilst powering a Strand Road–Riversway shuttle service.

1.2.2.6: Class 06 – Andrew Barclay and Sons

Builder
Andrew Barclay and Sons

Year Built
1956–1960

Engine
Gardner 8L3 rated at 204 hp @ 1200 rpm

Transmission
Mechanical

BR Fleet Numbers
11177–11186 (later D2400–2409); D2410–2444; TOPS = 06.001–010

06003 entered service as D2420 at Kittybrewster depot in February 1959 and was withdrawn from Eastfield depot in February 1981. It was transferred to Reading for Departmental Service in March 1981, being renumbered 97804 in May 1981. It was withdrawn in August 1985 and, following a short period in store, was sent for scrap in late September 1985. It became part of the HNRC collection between February 1987 and July 1998 and subsequently entered preservation when sold to the Shunters Heritage Trust, based at the Peak Railway (PR), during 2013.

06003 enters Barrow Hill's display yard (BHR) on 6 October 2002 whilst working a shuttle service in top 'n tail mode with Class 08 08899 during a gala event.

1.2.2.7: Class 07 – Ruston & Hornsby

Builder
Ruston & Hornsby

Year Built
1962

Engine
Paxman 6RPHL rated at 275 hp @ 1360 rpm

Transmission
Electric

BR Fleet Numbers
D2985–2998; TOPS = 07.001–014

History: This fleet of locomotives was ordered as replacement for the USA Class 0-6-0T used in Southampton Docks and the surrounding area.

07001 entered service as D2985 at Eastleigh depot in June 1966 from where it was withdrawn on 1 July 1977 and sold into industrial service. It later became part of the HNRC collection but was main-line registered for use as a spot hire locomotive until sold into preservation with the Heritage Shunters Trust in December 2012 who moved it to their base at Peak Rail (PR).

Top: 07001 is a display item during a Barrow Hill (BHR) diesel gala on 8 August 2009.

07005 entered service as D2989 at Eastleigh depot in June 1962 from where it was withdrawn on 1 July 1977 and sold into industrial service. It subsequently became part of the HNRC collection and was stored at the Battlefield Line (BL) until sold to the Great Central Railway (GCR) during early 2009.

Bottom: 07005 is noted stored in the GCR's Swithland Sidings on 13 November 2008 as it awaited its turn to be restored to working order.

1.2.2.8: Classes 08 thru 13 – British Railways

Builder
BR Crewe; BR Darlington: BR Derby; BR Doncaster; BR Horwich

Year Built
1952–1962

Engine
English Electric 6KT rated at 350/400 hp @ 630 rpm

Transmission
Electric

BR Fleet Numbers
13000–13366 (later D3000–D3366); D3367–4192; TOPS = 08.001–08.958
See also **History** (below)

History: Whilst the LMSR was developing its large shunter design in the 1930s, the other Pre-Grouping companies were also trialling similar locomotives but, when BR was created on 1 January 1948, the CME (Robert Riddles) elected to continue with the LMSR design as the BR Standard large shunting locomotive. In the early days of construction alternative engines were tested (namely Crossley (D3117–3126) and Blackstone (later Class 10) with a further trialling of BTH/GEC traction motors) but the final choice was the combination of English Electric engine and electrical equipment.

The Class 10 design with Blackstone engine and GEC electrical equipment proved sufficiently successful however that Doncaster built five batches (D3137–3151; D3439–3453; D3473–3502; D3612–3651; D4049–4094) totalling 146 locomotives which entered service at various Eastern Region depots.

Whilst nominally built as 'standard' locomotives there were variations introduced both during the build and afterwards, the prime example being the uprating of the engine from 350 hp to 400 hp. In a further development, twenty-six locomotives were built with higher gearing for operation on Southern Region lines (D3665–3671; D3719–21; D4099–4114; later TOPS = Class 09) whilst in 1992–3 a further twelve were rebuilt to this specification.

Earlier between 1985–1987, three locomotives were modified with cut-down cabs and renumbered 08993–08995 to allow them to replace Class 03 locomotive working on the reduced height Burry Port and Gwendraeth branch line in South Wales.

A final modification was made in February 1974 when three pairs of locomotives were converted by Doncaster Works to Master + slave units for heavy shunting in the new Tinsley marshalling yard; D4188 + D3698, D4190 + 4189 and D4187 + D3697 becoming D4500/01/02 respectively (later TOPS 13.003/01/02 respectively)

TOPS Classification: The introduction of TOPS in the late 1960s and its application to Fleet Operations from 1974 allowed these various sub-groups to be identified more clearly:

08.0 = Standard locomotive
08.9 = 3 locomotives with reduced cab height
09.0 = Locomotive with higher gearing
09.1 = Later conversion of locomotives with 110v electrical equipment; none preserved as at December 2016
09.2 = Later conversion of locomotives with 90v electrical equipment; none preserved as at December 2016
10.0 = Doncaster-built locomotives with Blackstone engine and GEC electrical equipment (TOPS numbers never carried)
11.0 = Original LMS locomotives (12033–12138); see Section 1.1.2
12.0 = Southern Region design based on LMS design (numbered 15211–15235 under BR fleet system); one example preserved as at December 2016 (TOPS numbers never carried)
13.0 = Master + slave units; locomotives cut up on withdrawal from service.

13265 entered service at Swansea Danycraig depot in August 1956 and was withdrawn from service at Cardiff Canton depot in September 1983 whence it was transferred to Swindon Works for scrapping. After a lengthy period in store it entered preservation with the Llangollen Railway (LR) in March 1986.

Opposite: **Recreating a scene from the past, 13265 performs shunting duties at the Pentre Felin yard of the LR on 26 March 2011.**

D3000 is a display item at Barrow Hill (BHR) on 5 October 2003 during a BHR diesel gala event.

Class doyen D3000 entered service as 13000 at Toton depot in October 1952 before transfer to Western Region depots including Bristol Bath Road from where it was withdrawn in November 1972 and sold to the National Coal Board (NCB) for further service. It entered preservation with the Southern Diesel Group (SDG) in December 1986 but passed through numerous owners until moving to Peak Rail (PR) in February 2011 where, as at 2016, it is undergoing restoration to working order.

08266 entered service as 13336 at Darnall depot in March 1957 and was withdrawn from Shirebrook depot in March 1985. It was moved to Swindon for scrapping whence it entered preservation with the Keighley & Worth Valley Railway (KWVR).

Right: **Fresh from overhaul and re-livery into Railfreight Grey colours, 08266 pilots recently bought Class 08/9 08995 Ashburnham out of Oxenholme (KWVR) on 18 June 2016 whilst working a service to Keighley on a Diesel Shunters gala event.**

D3586 entered service at Burton depot in November 1958 and was withdrawn from Leicester depot in September 1985 whence it was sent to Swindon Works for scrapping. It was bought by the Severn Valley Railway (SVR) and entered preservation in March 1986.

Left: **D3586 runs onto Bridgnorth depot (SVR) on 24 September 2005 whilst acting as shed pilot during the SVR's annual September Steam Gala.**

08911 entered service as D4141 at Carnforth depot in September 1962 and was withdrawn from Holbeck depot in February 2004 whence it entered service with the National Rail Museum (NRM) at York.

The locomotive was named *Matey* on 14 January 2007 in tribute to Ray Towell, a long serving member of the NRM staff who used the name for many of those with whom he came into contact. Sadly, Ray suffered a fatal heart attack on 28 March 2016 and was buried in his home town of Oakham.

Right: **08911 *Matey* stands inside the NRM at York on 23 November 2014.**

D4157 entered service at Lancaster Green Ayre depot in December 1962 and was withdrawn from Headquarters stock in June 2005 to pass into preservation with the Gloucestershire Warwickshire Railway (GWR).

Left: D4157 was hired to the NRM, which based it at its Shildon Centre and where it was noted on yard pilot duties on 19 October 2012.

D3937 entered service at Royston depot in March 1960 and was withdrawn from Landore depot in May 1989 whence it moved to the Fire Training College at Moreton-in-Marsh. It entered preservation with the Dean Forest Railway (DFR) in 1999.

Right: D3937 *Gladys* acts as shed pilot at Bridgnorth (SVR) on 21 September 2003 whilst on indefinite loan from the DFR.

08944 entered service as D4174 at Newport Ebbw Junction depot in August 1962 and was withdrawn from Old Oak Common depot in May 1998 whence it entered preservation with the East Lancashire Railway (ELR).

Left: 08.944 awaits departure from Bury (ELR) on 20 November 2004 with a service to Rawtenstall comprising Class 207 trainset 1305.

The line-up of locomotives in Buckley Wells yard on 28 August 2007 included (from left to right) 08.994 *Spirit of Innovation*; 08.995; 08.623; 08479 and 08.445.

The Class 08 has proved a successful design with BR and, following withdrawal from service, many examples had a successful second life either as contractors' locomotives or as motive power on heritage lines. One such line is the East Lancashire Railway (ELR) which offers facilities to the neighbouring Metrolink Network with which it has a rail connection.

In August 2007 the ELR site at Buckley Wells offered stabling facilities for rail-borne traffic during a major Metrolink engineering project, at the end of which an evening photographers' night session was arranged with the shunting locomotives used on the contract.

Class 09 D3666 entered traffic at Eastleigh depot in February 1959 and was withdrawn from Selhurst depot in September 1992 whence it entered service with the South Devon Railway (SDR). In 2010 the SDR bought 09.010 and intended using D3666 as spares but in February 2011 the locomotive was bought by GB Railfreight and returned to main line service as 09002.

D3666 lies stabled in SDR's Buckfastleigh yard on 20 July 2005

Class 09 D4100 entered service at Ashford depot in October 1961 and was withdrawn from Hither Green depot in February 2004. It remained in store until joining the HNRC collection in April 2010 before entering preservation with the Severn Valley Railway (SVR) in February 2013.

D4100 *Dick Hardy* pilots Class 08 D3022 out of Bewdley (SVR) on 21 May 2016 whilst powering the 10:10 Bewdley–Kidderminster service during the SVR's 2016 annual diesel gala.

Class 10 D4092 entered service at Darnall depot in May 1962 and was withdrawn from New England depot in September 1968 whence it entered industrial service with the NCB. It subsequently became part of the HNRC collection at the South Yorkshire Railway (SYR) before moving to the HNRC base at Barrow Hill (BHR).

D4092 is a display item at Barrow Hill (BHR) on 23 September 2015 during a diesel gala event.

Class 10 D4067 entered service at Darnall depot in April 1961 and was withdrawn from Shirebrook depot in December 1970 whence it entered industrial service with the NCB. It entered preservation with the Great Central Railway (GCR) in February 1980.

D4067 Margaret Ethel – Thomas Alfred Naylor lies stabled in the GCR's Loughborough Central yard on 29 January 2009.

Section 2:
Main Line Locomotives

When BR launched its Modernisation Plan in 1954 it only had the experience of six main line locomotives on which to base any decisions regarding future locomotive designs. These were the Derby-built 10000/1, the Southern Region's 10201–3 and the North British Locomotive Company 10800 built to a Derby specification. From these BR had understood that main line locomotives comprised three main parts – the engine, the transmission and the body shell to house the other two.

To test the combinations of elements BR proposed a pilot scheme covering a range of three locomotive types; Type A (800–1000 hp); Type B (1000–1500 hp) and Type C (2000 + hp) for which 171 locomotives were ordered (later supplemented by three locomotives with hydraulic transmission). Even as the first locomotives were being delivered, changes in government policy led to bulk orders being placed for locomotives and the introduction of designs that ultimately proved unsuitable for use. Despite this some designs had their supporters and from the mid-1970s the interest in preservation began to include main line diesel locomotives – both as a source of motive power for the burgeoning heritage line projects being promoted and by those wishing to see certain designs continue operating on the main line.

The Pilot Scheme orders that were placed encompassed the following design combinations:

TYPE A – later Type 1 – for light passenger and trip freight duties
20: D8000–8019 English Electric build with English Electric engine and electric transmission

10: D8200–8209 British Thomson Houston/Yorkshire Engine Co build with Paxman engine and BTH electric transmission

10: D8400–8409 North British Loco build with Paxman engine and GEC electric transmission.

TYPE B – later Type 2 – for mixed traffic duties
20: D5000–5019 BR Derby build with Sulzer engine and AEI/BTH electric transmission

20: D5300–5319 Birmingham RC&W build with Sulzer engine and Crompton Parkinson electric transmission

20: D5500–5519 Brush Traction build with Mirrlees Bickerton & Day engine and Brush electric transmission

20: D5700–5719 Metropolitan Vickers build with Crossley engine and Metropolitan Vickers electric transmission

10: D5900–5909 English Electric build with Napier engine and English Electric electric transmission

10: D6100–6109 North British Loco build with NBL/MAN engine and GEC electric transmission

6: D6300–6305 North British Loco build with NBL/MAN engine and NBL/Voith hydraulic transmission

TYPE C – later Type 4 – for express passenger duties
10: D1–10 BR Derby build with Sulzer engine and Crompton Parkinson electric transmission

10: D200–209 English Electric build with English Electric engine and English Electric electric transmission

5: D600–604 North British Loco build with NBL/MAN engines and NBL/Voith hydraulic transmission

3: D800–802 BR Swindon build with Maybach engines and Mekydro hydraulic transmission

The National Traction Plan of 1968 encompassed a review of diesel locomotive operation to date and quickly identified locomotive designs that could be withdrawn as unreliable, unsuited to future operations or were fitted with hydraulic transmission which was officially considered to be redundant following BR's decision to adopt electric transmission as standard. Whilst most locomotives were scrapped, many were saved as the glut of diesel locomotives occurred concurrent with the pool of steam locomotives becoming exhausted whilst many nascent heritage lines were looking for motive power. The way forward was indicated in 1977 with the purchase of Class 42 D821 *Greyhound* by a small group that subsequently became the Diesel Traction Group (DTG), funded through private finance, and the purchase of Class 35 D7017 by the Diesel & Electric Preservation Group (DEPG) funded through public subscription. Subsequent locomotive preservation projects have continued up to the present day (December 2016) with some bought for a return to main line operation.

NOTE: Since privatisation in 1994 locomotives have been allocated by sector rather than depot and, once withdrawn, have been stored until tender lists have identified locomotives for sale; once purchased locomotives have remained stored until a suitable base for restoration/operation can be found. This has made it difficult to provide accurate details of preservation dates but attempts have been made to identify the dates of entry into preservation and the current location of illustrated locomotives.

Pilot Scheme Type A Class Doyen D8000 entered service at Devons Road Bow depot in August 1957 as the first Pilot Scheme locomotive to be delivered and was withdrawn from Toton depot in October 1980. It was moved to Swindon Works for storage and entered preservation with the NRM in October 1981, initially moving to St Rollox Works for asbestos removal.

Left: D8000 is loaned out to heritage sites on occasion as on 15 July 2007 when it made a guest appearance at Barrow Hill (BHR) to commemorate the 50th anniversary of the design being introduced to service; it is here seen pilotting sister locomotive D8001 on the shuttle service as they depart from the Barrow Hill platform.

Pilot Scheme Type C Class Doyen D200 was released in March 1958 to Doncaster for trials after which it was transferred to Stratford depot and was withdrawn from Longsight depot in August 1981. It moved to Kingmoor depot on 6 August 1981 for long term storage until 30 April 1983 when it moved to Crewe Works then to Toton depot on 10 May 1983 for overhaul and return to traffic. It entered preservation when presented to the NRM on 16 April 1988 following official withdrawal from BR service.

Right: D200 lies stabled under cover in an annexe of the NRM at York on 11 July 2013.

Pilot Scheme Type B Class Doyen D5300 entered service at Hornsey depot in July 1958 and was withdrawn from Inverness depot in October 1993. It was sold into preservation in May 1995 and visited St Rollox Works for asbestos removal before continuing to Barrow Hill (BHR) where its owner undertook the restoration to working condition.

Left: D5300 bears its TOPS number of 26007 as it stands in Barrow Hill display yard (BHR) on 22 August 2008 forming part of the RailPower 2008 display.

2.1: Type 1 Designs

The Type 1 (Pilot Scheme Type A) designs were based on the experience gained from LMSR Derby-specified 10800 which had been designed for use on duties currently operated by steam class 3 locomotives – namely trip workings and local passenger duties.

In the event much of the passenger work was later worked by multiple unit (MU) trainsets, the local trip workings disappeared as the freight services were lost to road transport and the selected engine of some designs proved unsatisfactory in service – as would have been identified sooner had the original Pilot Scheme been continued to its proposed end date.

That said, some 'failed' designs had garnered sufficient interest that class members have entered preservation with dedicated support teams who work to restore locomotives that had had a part to play in the early days of BR's Modernisation Plan.

2.1.1: Class 14 – BR Swindon Works

Builder
BR Swindon

Year Built
1964–1965

Engine
Paxman 6YJX rated at 650 hp @ 1500 rpm

Transmission
Hydraulic

BR Fleet Numbers
D9500–9555; TOPS = Class 14 (TOPS numbers never carried)

History: This class was originally specified to replace the various Western Region 0-6-0PT designs as part of the plan to eradicate steam from South Wales routes west of the Severn Tunnel but, even as they were being built, their proposed duties were disappearing in the changed operating environment following both Beeching closures and competition from road transport during the 1960s.

In 1968 D9539 was demonstrated to industrial concerns leading to the sale of 48 locomotives into industry from which 19 were subsequently preserved; many received the modifications that BR would have undertaken had they retained them in service, thus in preservation they proved to be the reliable workhorses that BR had intended them to be.

D9539 entered service at Cardiff Canton depot in April 1965 but moved to Hull depot in May 1967 from where it was withdrawn in April 1968. Demonstrated at BSC Harlaxton (by Grantham) in October 1968, it was sold to industry (British Steel Corporation) immediately after the event and led to the ultimate sale of 48 class members to industry. It entered preservation with the Gloucester Warwickshire Railway (GWR) in February 1983 and was subsequently sold to a private owner who transferred it to the Ribble Steam Railway (RSR), its current home base as at December 2016, in July 2005.

Above: D9539 poses at the RSR's Riversway Siding on 5 April 2014 during an evening photographers' charter.

Opposite: In 2014 the East Lancashire Railway (ELR) hosted an anniversary gala to celebrate fifty years since the first locomotive (D9500) had been released to traffic and 10 of the 19 preserved locomotives were operated during the event. During the gala D9523 failed with serious mechanical failure and missed the celebratory operation of the Saturday evening 'Beerex' which was operated with all the locomotives. The 'Beerex' was noted passing Burrs on 26 July 2014 powered by D9531 *Ernest*; D9520; D9513; D9555; D9521; D9526; D9539; D9524 (as 14.901); and D9537.

2.1.2: Class 15 – British Thomson Houston

Builder
Yorkshire Engine Company; Clayton Equipment Company

Year Built
1957–61

Engine
Paxman 16YHXL rated at 800 hp @ 1250 rpm

Transmission
Electric

BR Fleet Numbers
D8200–8243; TOPS = Class 15 (TOPS numbers never carried)

History: The Pilot Scheme order for D8200–8209 was built by the Yorkshire Engine Company but the follow-on orders were completed by associate company Clayton Equipment Company. This proved to be the most successful of the Type A designs fitted with Paxman engines but still fell victim to the rationalisation of the National Traction Plan in 1968.

D8233 entered service at Stratford depot in August 1960 and was withdrawn from Finsbury Park depot in February 1969 and transferred to Departmental Stock as an unpowered Carriage Heating Unit. It entered preservation with the South Yorkshire Railway (SYR) at Meadowhall in 1984 since when it has passed through various ownerships until being moved to the East Lancashire Railway (ELR) in February 2006 where, as at December 2016, its restoration to operational condition continues.

D8233 stands in Crewe Heritage Centre (CHC) on 11 June 2005 awaiting restoration which began the following year when it was transferred to the ownership of the Class 15 Preservation Society and moved to a new base on the ELR.

2.1.3: Class 17 – Clayton Equipment Company

Builder
Clayton Equipment Company; Beyer Peacock Company

Year Built
1962–1965

Engine
2 x Paxman 6ZHXL rated at 450 hp @ 1500 rpm (D8586–7 with Rolls Royce 'D' rated at 450 hp)

Transmission
Electric

BR Fleet Numbers
D8500–8616; Tops = Class 17 (TOPS numbers never carried)

TOPS Classification: The introduction of TOPS in the late 1960s and its application to Fleet Operations from 1974 allowed these various sub-groups to be identified more clearly, although no class member ever received a TOPS fleet number:

17/1 = D8500–8585 built with Paxman engines and GEC electrical equipment
17/2 = D8586–8587 built with Rolls Royce engines and GEC electrical equipment
17/3 = D8588–8616 Built by Beyer Peacock with Paxman engines and Crompton Parkinson electrical equipment

D8568 entered service at Haymarket depot in January 1964 and was withdrawn from Polmadie depot in October 1971. Following a lengthy period in store it was sold to industry in September 1972 whence it entered preservation with the Diesel Traction Group (DTG) in February 1983 based on the North Yorkshire Moors Railway (NYMR). In early 1992 it was transferred to a new base on the Chinnor & Princes Risborough Railway (CPRR) where it arrived in April 1992 and from where it makes occasional visits to other heritage lines.

History: In the early 1960s BR specified a standard design for Type 1 locomotives that included a central cab and commissioned a development of the Class 15 design from the Clayton Equipment Company. Even before the first locomotive was trialled in July 1962 follow-on orders were placed that ultimately proved disastrous. The class suffered mechanical problems, particularly with the engines, and proved so unreliable that all were withdrawn by the end of 1971.

D8568 climbs past Hayes Bridge (SVR) on 2 October 2015 with the 13:47 Kidderminster–Bridgnorth service during the SVR's annual diesel gala when D8568 was the 'guest' locomotive for the event.

2.1.4: Class 20 – English Electric Company

Builder
English Electric (Vulcan Works); English Electric (Robert Stephenson Hawthorn (RSH) Darlington)

Year Built
1957–68

Engine
English Electric 8SVT rated at 1000 hp @ 850 rpm

Transmission
Electric

BR Fleet Numbers
D8000–8199; 8300–8327; TOPS = 20001–20228

History: The Pilot Scheme order for D8000–8019 was followed by further orders ending at D8127 but when the Class 17s proved unreliable in service an order for a further 100 locomotives (D8128–8199; D8300–8327) was placed by BR. The success of the class was further improved by the ability of coupling locomotives nose-to-nose to provide a 2000 hp traction unit with a cab at both ends whilst the eight axles provided superior braking power when working non-brake-fitted trains – especially in the Nottinghamshire coalfield.

TOPS Classification: The introduction of TOPS in the late 1960s and its application to Fleet Operations from 1974 allowed various sub-groups to be identified:

20/0 = Standard fleet
20/3 = 20301–20305 dedicated to Railfreight duty at Peak Forest but the project was cancelled and the locomotives regained their standard fleet numbers
20/3 = 20301–20315 refurbished locomotives bought by Direct Rail Services (DRS) in 1995–96
20/9 = 20901–20906 refurbished locomotives bought by Hunslet-Barclay for weed-killing services in 1989 and subsequently bought by DRS and, later, Harry Needle Railway Company (HNRC).

D8059 entered service at Darnall depot in May 1961 and was withdrawn from Toton depot in May 1993 whilst D8188 entered service with D16 (Nottingham Division) in January 1967 and was withdrawn from Toton depot in January 1990. Both locos suffered long term storage until entering preservation in 1996 with the Somerset & Dorset Locomotive Company based at Yeovil. As at December 2016 both locomotives are on hire to the Severn Valley Railway (SVR).

The second man of D8188 prepares to surrender the single line token at Bewdley (SVR) as it enters the station, paired with sister locomotive D8059, whilst working the 11:18 Bridgnorth–Kidderminster service on 21 May 2016 during the SVR's annual diesel gala.

D8087 entered service at Eastfield depot in September 1961 and was withdrawn from Bescot depot in April 1995 whence it became part of the Contract Fleet employed in such projects as the Channel Tunnel. It entered preservation, following private purchase, at the East Lancashire Railway (ELR) in June 1999.

Above: D8087 crosses the River Irwell at Summerseat (ELR) on 30 August 2003 whilst approaching Summerseat station with the 10:00 Rawtenstall–Bury service.

D8132 entered service at Tinsley depot in March 1966 but quickly transferred to Barrow Hill depot to replace the ailing Class 17 locomotives that were subsequently transferred elsewhere; it was withdrawn from Bescot depot in November 1995 whence it became part of the Contract Fleet employed in such projects as the Channel Tunnel. It was subsequently sold to DRS then to HNRC for spares but HNRC opted to restore it to operating condition and, as at December 2016, it is one of the pool of locomotives hired to GBRf for stock transfers.

Below: D8132 works the shuttle service at Barrow Hill (BHR) in top 'n tail mode with Class 73/1 73138 during a diesel gala held on 8 July 2006.

D8118 entered service at Polmadie depot in March 1962 and was withdrawn from Bescot depot in December 1995 following a period of storage which continued until entering preservation with the South Devon Railway (SDR) in December 1999. D8118 returned to mainline service when sold to Harry Needle Railway Company (HNRC) in April 2011 and subsequently became one of the pool of locomotives hired to GB Railfreight (GBRf) for stock transfers.

Above: Operating as 20118 *Saltburn by Sea* and bearing Railfreight livery, D8118 runs alongside the River Dart (SDR) on 20 July 2005 whilst working a Buckfastleigh–Totnes service.

20110 is piloted by 20087 as they approach Oakworth (KWVR) on 6 June 2008 whilst working the 12:00 Oxenhope–Keighley service during the KWVR's annual diesel gala.

20110 entered service as D8110 at Eastfield depot in January 1962 and was withdrawn from Toton depot in September 1990 to enter storage. It was bought by the South Devon Diesel Group (SDDG) and entered preservation at the SDR in 1991. It was subsequently purchased by HNRC and, as at December 2016, was based at the East Lancashire Railway (ELR) with reports that a move elsewhere was being negotiated.

2.2: Type 2 Designs

The Type 2 (Pilot Scheme Type B) designs were specified as mixed traffic locomotives, given that the current thinking was that a 1600 hp engine was considered equivalent to a Class 5 steam locomotive. Many of these designs proved successful in service, although some designs that might have been identified as 'failures' by the Pilot Scheme were still retained longer than many expected.

Such was their success that examples of each design were bought for preservation once withdrawn from BR service and proved useful assets to the operating heritage line(s).

2.2.1: Class 23 – English Electric

Builder
English Electric (Vulcan)

Year Built
1959

Engine
Deltic T9–29 rated at 1100 hp @ 1600 rpm

Transmission
Electric

BR Fleet Numbers
D5900–5909; D5910; TOPS = Class 23 (TOPS numbers never carried)

History: This Pilot Scheme design proved to be the only English Electric Company failure from all the designs it proffered for consideration as part of the Pilot Scheme and, despite a rebuilding in the mid-1960s, all were withdrawn from service by the end of the 1960s.

When the class was scrapped there was one power unit left which was donated to the National Rail Museum (NRM) at York. In 2001, the NRM was approached by a group seeking to recreate the design by converting a Class 37 bodyshell to that of a Class 23. The NRM agreed to sell the engine which was subsequently moved to Barrow Hill (BHR) and where, in 2008, a successful start-up was achieved. The full project was launched to the public in 2010 with advice that progress would depend on funding and, as at December 2016, progress on remodelling the bodyshell still continues.

Progress on display at Barrow Hill (BHR) on 6 February 2014 as the bodyshell of Class 37/3 37372 is remodelled to create Class 23 D5910.

2.2.2: Classes 24 thru 25 – British Railways

Builder
BR (Crewe); BR (Derby); BR (Darlington); Beyer Peacock

Year Built
1958–1967

Engine
Sulzer 6LDA28A rated at 1160 hp @ 750 rpm (Class 24); Sulzer 6LDA28B rated at 1250 hp @750 rpm (Class 25)

Transmission
Electric

BR Fleet Numbers
D5000–5150 (TOPS = 24001–24150); D5151–5299 (TOPS = 25001–149); D7500–7677 (TOPS = 25150–25327); 25901–25912

History: The Pilot Scheme order for D5000–5019 was followed by further orders which ultimately resulted in the production of 477 locomotives that followed the old Midland Railway concept of using single locomotives for local freight duties and coupling two locomotives to operate in multiple to work heavier freight or passenger duties. The locomotives worked all over the BR network and when withdrawn from service those locomotives which entered preservation were still found to be a useful asset to their new owners.

Notes of interest:
1. D7667 was the 1000th diesel locomotive built by Derby Works
2. D7598–7677 were initially subcontracted to Beyer Peacock but that company's bankruptcy in 1966 saw the build finish at D7659 and the build for D7660–7677 returned to Derby Works

TOPS Classification: The introduction of TOPS in the late 1960s and its application to Fleet Operations from 1974 allowed various sub-groups to be identified but, due to the large number of locomotives, they were not given separate sub-group numbering:

24/0 = D5000–5050 original build
24/1 = D5051–5150 revised build to reduce weight
25/0 = D5151–5175 built with Sulzer 6LDA28B engine
25/1 = D5176–5232; D7568–7597 as 25/0 with revised roof mountings and AEI traction motors
25/2 = D5233–5299; D7500–7567 with revised body styling and removal of gangway doors
25/3 = D7598–7677 with revised electrical equipment
25/9 = 25901–25912 was a dedicated pool created from surviving Class 25/3 locomotives at the end of 1985 for a traffic contract that failed to materialise.

Class 24/1 D5054 entered service at March depot in January 1959 and was withdrawn from Crewe Diesel depot in July 1976 whence it was transferred to Departmental stock. It entered preservation with the Bury Transport Museum, associated with the East Lancashire Railway (ELR), in October 1983 and, as at December 2016, is still based at the ELR.

Left: D5054 awaits departure from Irwell Vale (ELR) on 5 July 2003 whilst working the 09:40 Bury–Rawtenstall service.

Below Left: D5054 bears Load Haul livery as it stands at Ramsbottom (ELR) on 16 March 2002 whilst working the 14:00 Rawtenstall–Bury service.

Below Right: D5054 carries the name *Phil Southern* (an ELR volunteer) on 23 September 2015 as it awaits its turn to receive a heavy overhaul at the Barrow Hill (BHR) workshops of preservation supporter Harry Needle.

Class 25/3 25313 entered service as D7663 at Willesden depot in November 1966 and was withdrawn from Crewe Diesel depot in March 1987 whence it was transferred to Vic Berry at Leicester for scrapping. It was sold from there and entered preservation with the Llangollen Railway (LR) in June 1988.

Left: 25313 lies stabled in the diesel line at Llangollen (LR) on 31 May 2008.

Class 25/1 D5185 entered service at Toton depot in May 1963 and was withdrawn from Crewe Diesel depot in March 1987 from where it was transferred to Vic Berry at Leicester for scrapping. It was sold from there and entered preservation with the Northampton & Lamport Railway (N&LR) in July 1988 and subsequently moved to the Great Central Railway (GCR) in 2002.

Right: D5185 stands in Quorn yard (GCR) on 15 October 2009.

Class 25/2 D7523 entered service at Toton depot in January 1965 and was withdrawn from Crewe Diesel depot in March 1987 whence it was transferred to Vic Berry at Leicester for scrapping. It was sold from there and entered preservation with the Dean Forest Railway (DFR) in July 1989 with subsequent moves to the West Somerset Railway (WSR) then to the Epping Ongar Railway (EOR) where it is based as at December 2016.

Left: D7523, named *John F Kennedy*, stands in Williton yard (WSR) on 20 March 2011.

Class 25/3 D7612 entered service at Eastfield depot in April 1966 and was withdrawn from Kingmoor depot in March 1987. After lengthy storage it entered preservation with the East Lancashire Railway (ELR) in September 1989 after asbestos removal at MC Metals in Glasgow and was subsequently sold to the South Devon Railway (SDR) where it is currently based as at December 2016.

Left: D7612 pilots Class 25/1 25059 as they approach Oakworth (KWVR) on 6 June 2008 whilst working the 15:00 Oxenhope–Keighley service during the KWVR's annual diesel gala.

Class 25/3 25322 entered service as D7672 at Willesden depot in February 1967 and was withdrawn from Kingmoor depot in March 1987 to enter Departmental service and transfer to Holbeck depot for training purposes. It was withdrawn from stock in April 1991 and entered preservation at the Churnet Valley Railway (CVR) in May 1991.

Right: 25322 *Tamworth Castle* lies stored at Cheddleton (CVR) on 6 June 2012 awaiting its turn for restoration.

Class 25/3 D7628 entered service at Wath depot (sub-shed of Tinsley depot) in September 1965 and was withdrawn from Crewe Diesel depot in March 1987 whence it was moved to Vic Berry at Leicester for scrapping. It was sold from there and entered preservation at the North Yorkshire Moors Railway (NYMR) in January 1988 once asbestos removal had been completed.

Left: D7628 pilots Class 26/2 26038 into Haworth (KWVR) on 26 April 2013 whilst working the 10:25 Oxenhope–Keighley service during the KWVR's annual diesel gala.

Class 25/1 25059 entered service as D5209 at Toton depot in June 1963 and was withdrawn from Crewe Diesel depot in March 1987 whence it was transferred to Vic Berry at Leicester for scrapping. It was sold from there and entered preservation at the Keighley & Worth Valley Railway (KWVR) in October 1987.

Class 25/1 25067 entered service as D5217 at Toton depot in August 1963 and was withdrawn from Cricklewood depot in December 1982 whence it was transferred to Vic Berry at Leicester for scrapping. It was sold from there and entered preservation at the Mid-Hants Railway (MHR) in November 1985; subsequent moves have seen it based at the Battlefield Line (BL) as at December 2016.

Right: 25059 pilots D5217 on 8 June 2014 as they prepare to leave Oakworth (KWVR) with the 12:20 Keighley–Oxenhope service during the KWVR's annual diesel gala.

Below Right: 25059 climbs towards Oakworth (KWVR) on 6 June 2008 whilst working the 12:45 Keighley–Oxenhope service during the KWVR's annual diesel gala.

Below Left: D5217 pilots 25059 as they curve into Oakworth (KWVR) on 8 June 2014 with the 13:10 Oxenhope–Keighley service during the KWVR's annual diesel gala.

Class 24/1 D5081 entered traffic at March depot in March 1960 and was withdrawn from Crewe Diesel depot in October 1980 from where it entered preservation at Steamport (Southport). Although the official withdrawal date was given as 5 October 1980, the locomotive had failed during a visit to Steamport (Southport) in September 1980 and a Steamport member had subsequently purchased the locomotive in situ hence the official withdrawal date being after the sale date.

D5081 curves into Ramsbottom (ELR) on 6 July 2012 whilst working the 10:56 Rawtenstall–Heywood service during the ELR's annual diesel gala.

Class 24/1 D5061 entered service at March depot in January 1960 and was withdrawn from Crewe Diesel depot in August 1975 whence it entered Departmental service. It was withdrawn in December 1987 and, after being stored, moved under its own power to Vic Berry at Leicester for scrapping in July 1988 where the subsequent bankruptcy of the company prevented its destruction. It entered preservation in July 1991 at the Midland Railway Centre (MRC) but then transferred to the North Yorkshire Moors Railway (NYMR) where, as at December 2016, it is currently based.

D5061 is stabled in Grosmont station (NYMR) on 25 July 2009 as it awaits its next duty.

2.2.3: Classes 26 thru 27 – Birmingham RC&W

Builder
Birmingham RC&W Company

Year Built
1958–1962

Engine
Sulzer 6LDA28A rated at 1160 hp @ 750 rpm (Class 26); Sulzer 6LDA28B rated at 1250 hp @750 rpm (Class 27)

Transmission
Electric

BR Fleet Numbers
D5300–5346 (TOPS = 26001–26046); D5347–5415 (TOPS = 27001–27044 (later 27066)); 27101–27112; 27201–27212
See also TOPS Classification

History: The Pilot Scheme order for D5300–5319 was followed by further orders which ultimately resulted in the production of 116 locomotives with the first allocation being to Hornsey for Kings Cross suburban duties. Following trials with D5311 and the subsequent deliveries of Class 30 (later Class 31) locomotives the fleet was transferred to Edinburgh and subsequent deliveries of Class 26 went directly to Inverness depot for Highland Line duties.

As further follow-on orders were being prepared, Sulzer introduced the uprated 6LDA28B engine that was subsequently specified for the next order which later became designated Class 27. The early build of Class 27 locomotives were based at Eastfield depot for West Highland Lines duties whilst subsequent batches were based at Thornaby and Cricklewood depots.

In the early 1970s the Class 27 fleet was transferred to Scottish depots and some class members were refurbished for push-pull workings between Edinburgh and Glasgow but, when subsequently replaced by Class 47/Driving Trailer combinations, the displaced locomotives gained fleet numbers 27045–27066 and returned to 'normal' duties.

Notes of interest
1. D5300–5306 were modified with air brakes and slow speed equipment in 1969 to work MGR services to Cockenzie Power Station; they became designated 26/0 whilst the remaining thirteen members of this group were reclassified Class 26/1 and Class 26/1 became Class 26/2.
2. Class 27/1 originally allotted 27101–124 but twelve locomotives were subsequently redesignated Class 27/2 when a later decision was taken to fit electric heating.

TOPS Classification: The introduction of TOPS in the late 1960s and its application to Fleet Operations from 1974 allowed various sub-groups to be identified:

26/0 = D5300–5319; later D5300–5306 only once refurbished for MGR duties
26/1 = D5320–5346; later D5307–5319 once D5300–5306 converted
26/2 = D5320–5346 once D5300–5306 converted
27/0 = D5347–5415
27/1 = 12 locomotives converted to push-pull with steam heat; when restored to 'original' condition renumbered to 27045–27056
27/2 = 12 locomotives converted to push-pull with electric heat; when restored to 'original' condition surviving locomotives renumbered to 27057–27066.

A scene from preservation at Barrow Hill (BHR) on 12 August 2006 sees 26011 and class doyen D5300/26007 in various stages of restoration by their respective owners.

Class 26/0 D5301 entered service at Hornsey depot in September 1958 and was withdrawn from Inverness depot in October 1993. Following a lengthy period in store it entered preservation with the Lakeside & Haverthwaite Railway (LHR) in September 1996.

Left: **D5301 approaches Newby Bridge (LHR) on 15 November 2003 whilst working the 11:45 Haverthwaite–Lakeside service during a Diesel Day event.**

Class 26/0 26004 entered service as D5304 at Hornsey depot in September 1958 and was withdrawn from Inverness depot in November 1992 whence it entered preservation at the Bo'ness & Kinneil Railway (BKR).

Right: **26004 bears Railfreight Coal decals as it stands in Bo'ness station (BKR) on 31 March 2002 awaiting its next duty.**

Class 26/1 D5310 entered service at Hornsey depot in January 1959 and was withdrawn from Inverness depot in December 1992 whence it entered preservation at the Bo'ness & Kinneil Railway (BKR). It was subsequently sold to the Llangollen Railway (LR) where it is currently based as at December 2016.

Left: **D5310 pilots Class 26/2 26024 on 4 July 2007 as they depart from Ramsbottom (ELR) with the 11:15 Heywood–Rawtenstall service during the ELR's annual diesel gala.**

Class 26/2 26038 entered service as D5338 at Haymarket depot in August 1959 and was withdrawn from Inverness depot in October 1992 whence it was bought by Tom Clift and moved to the South Yorkshire Railway (SYR) at Meadowhall in December 1994. It subsequently moved to Cardiff for restoration when Tom Clift became head of Cardiff Valleys Railways. His unexpected death shortly before D5338/26038 completed its restoration led to the locomotive being named *Tom Clift 1954–2012* in his honour.

The locomotive is based at the Bo'ness & Kinneil Railway (BKR) as at December 2016 and from where it visits other heritage lines.

Left: 26038 *Tom Clift 1954–2012* calls at Irwell Vale (ELR) on 4 July 2015 whilst working the 12:33 Heywood–Rawtenstall service during the ELR's annual diesel gala.

Right: Class 26/1 D5310 curves away from Glyndyfrdwy on 2 October 2010 whilst working the 11:30 Carrog–Llangollen Goods Jn Demonstration Freight during a diesel day event.

Left: 26038 approaches Haworth (KWVR) on 26 April 2013 whilst working the 10:25 Oxenhope–Keighley service during the KWVR's annual diesel gala.

Class 26/1 26024 entered service as D5324 at Haymarket depot in May 1959 and was withdrawn from Inverness depot in October 1992 whence it entered preservation at the Bo'ness & Kinneil Railway (BKR).

Left: 26024 climbs past Heaps Bridge (ELR) on 9 July 2000 whilst working the 11:37 Bury–Heywood service in top 'n tail mode with Class 42 D832 *Onslaught* during the ELR's annual diesel gala.

Class 27/0 doyen 27001 entered service as D5347 at Thornton Junction depot in June 1961 and was withdrawn from Eastfield depot in July 1987 whence it entered preservation at the Bo'ness & Kinneil Railway (BKR).

Right: 27001 shunts stock at Bo'ness (BKR) on 24 February 2009 in preparation for a photographic charter being held later that day.

Class 27/0 27024 entered service as D5370 at Thornaby depot in January 1962 and was withdrawn from Eastfield depot in July 1987 to enter Departmental stock in June 1989. It was withdrawn from stock in December 1989 and entered preservation with the Caledonian Railway Diesel Group at the Caledonian Railway (CR) based at Brechin.

Left: 27024 approaches Newby Bridge (LHR) on 16 November 2008 whilst working a Haverthwaite–Lakeside service during a Diesel Day event; the locomotive had been exchanged with resident Class 26/0 D5301 for a brief period hence its appearance on the LHR.

D5401 passes Fisherman's Crossing (LR) on 6 October 2007 whilst working the 13:00 Llangollen–Carrog service during an LR Diesel Day event.

Class 27/0 D5401 entered service at Cricklewood depot in July 1962 and was withdrawn from Eastfield depot in February 1987 whence it was moved to Vic Berry at Leicester for scrapping. It was sold from there to the Northampton & Lamport Railway (NLR) in March 1988 and subsequently moved to the Great Central Railway (GCR) where it is currently based as at December 2016. During its BR service this locomotive also operated as 27112 before reverting to 27056.

D5386 carries BR Corporate Blue livery as it crosses the River Irwell at Summerseat (ELR) on 13 September 2003 whilst working the 11:20 Bury–Rawtenstall service.

Class 27/0 D5386 entered service at Cricklewood depot in May 1962 and was withdrawn from service at Eastfield depot in July 1987 whence it entered preservation at the North Norfolk Railway (NNR) with a subsequent move to the Dean Forest Railway (DFR). During 2016 it was sold to Harry Needle Railway Company (HNRC) and as at December 2016 is undergoing overhaul at HNRC's base at Barrow Hill (BHR). During its BR service this locomotive also operated as 27103/27212 before reverting to 27066.

2.2.4: Class 28 – Metropolitan Vickers

Builder
Metropolitan Vickers

Year Built
1958–1959

Engine
Crossley 8-cylinder HST V8 rated at 1200 hp @ 625 rpm

Transmission
Electric

BR Fleet Numbers
D5700–5719; TOPS = Class 28 (TOPS numbers never carried)

History: The Pilot Scheme order for D5700–5719 was placed to trial both a 2-stroke engine design and identify whether a Co-Bo wheel arrangement would reduce axle-loads in any way. In practice the engine proved troublesome and the fleet was transferred to the Furness Coast area to end its days.

Notes of interest
1. In 1963 discussions began with English Electric to replace the Crossley engines with an English Electric 12SVT engine but the decision to re-engine the 262 locomotives of Class 30 with the same engine saw the project cancelled.

TOPS Classification: The introduction of TOPS in the late 1960s and its application to Fleet Operations from 1974 saw the class identified as Class 28 but no locomotive survived to carry a TOPS Fleet Number.

D5705 entered service at Derby depot in July 1958 and was withdrawn from D10 (Carlisle) Division in September 1968 to enter Departmental service with the Research Department before becoming a carriage heating unit at Bristol. It entered preservation in 1980 and was stored at Swindon until resold and moved to Peak Rail (PR) in March 1986 from where it moved to the East Lancashire Railway (ELR) in January 1997 for its restoration to continue.

D5705 rests in the workshops of Crewe Works on 11 September 2005 after being used to demonstrate lifting techniques during the Crewe Works Open Day.

2.2.5: Class 31 – Brush Traction

Builder
Brush Traction

Year Built
1957–1962

Engine
English Electric 12SVT rated at 1470 hp @ 850 rpm

Transmission
Electric

BR Fleet Numbers
D5500–5519 (TOPS = 31001–019); D5520–5699; D5800–5862; TOPS = 31101–31327; 31400–31470; 31500–31570 (with gaps)

History: The Pilot Scheme order for D5500–5519 found favour in the Eastern Region (ER) of BR and further orders followed that ultimately resulted in the production of 262 locomotives. The first twenty locomotives were originally fitted with a Mirrlees Bickerton & Day JSVT12 engine rated at 1250 hp @ 850 rpm but the production batches had different control equipment and an engine uprating to 1365 hp @ 900 rpm whilst some batches were further uprated to develop 1600 hp @ 950 rpm. In 1964 major problems were identified with the engine and the fleet was subsequently re-engined with English Electric 12SVT engines between 1965 and 1969; this improved reliability to the point that class members are still working on the main line as at December 2016.

Notes of interest:
1. D5545 was fitted from new with a 1600 hp engine leading to D5655–5670 being fitted with this engine from new for use in East Anglia and identifying the need for the higher power range that led to the specification/production of the Class 37 design.
2. D5835 was trialled from new with an engine rated at 2000hp @ 950 rpm and operated on Type 4 diagrams but nothing came of the trials.
3. In the early 1970s, the introduction of Electric Train Heating (ETH) saw the conversion of random locomotives, that were remembered under the TOPS classification in stages to provide pre-warming facilities as part of ecs (empty coaching stock) duties. The locomotives later found use on passenger services leading to the further conversion of 31425–31470 in stages as the locomotives replaced ageing multiple unit trainsets on secondary passenger duties during the 1980s.

TOPS Classification: The introduction of TOPS in the late 1960s and its application to Fleet Operations from 1974 allowed various sub-groups to be identified:

30.0 = D5500–5519 with original Mirrlees engine (no TOPS number ever carried)
30.1 = D5520–5699; 5800–5862 with original Mirrlees engine (no TOPS number ever carried)
31.0 = D5500–5519 (TOPS = 31001–31019)
31.1 = D5520–5699; 5800–5862 (TOPS=31101–31327)
31.4 = 31400–31470 Random locomotives fitted with Electric Train Heating equipment (ETH)
31.5 = Class 31.4 locomotives transferred to Civil Engineers Department with ETH equipment removed/disconnected
31.6 = 31601–31602 Class 31.1 locomotives fitted with through ETH cables.

D5500 stands in the NRM at York on 9 November 2013 in the BR Corporate Blue livery with TOPS number 31018 as borne at withdrawal.

Class 31/0 doyen D5500 entered service at Stratford depot in October 1957 from where it was withdrawn in July 1976 to enter preservation with the National Rail Museum (NRM) in York. In the early days of preservation the locomotive was hired to heritage lines but the presence of asbestos has reduced the frequency to the point that, as at December 2016, the locomotive is now maintained as a static exhibit at York.

Class 31/4 D5600 entered service at Hornsey depot in March 1960 and was withdrawn from Bescot depot in November 1995. It entered preservation at the East Lancashire Railway (ELR) in December 1999 after lengthy storage but was subsequently moved by its owner to the Embsay & Bolton Abbey Railway (EBAR) in September 2007 where it is based as at December 2016.

Right: D5600 works in top 'n tail mode with Class 55 'Deltic' 55022 *Royal Scots Grey* as it approaches Ramsbottom (ELR) on 11 November 2006 with the 11:15 Rawtenstall–Heywood service.

Below: Restored to original lined green livery, D5600 departs from Summerseat (ELR) on 20 November 2004 whilst working the 10:05 Heywood–Rawtenstall service.

Class 31/1 D5830 entered service at Darnall depot in January 1962 and was withdrawn from Bescot depot in February 1998. It was bought to provide spares for class 31/4 31418 then under restoration by the Type 1 Locomotive Society at the Great Central Railway (GCR) but its condition was found to be better resulting in 31418 being sold on and D5830 being restored.

Opposite Page: Bearing the Golden Ochre livery once applied to D5579, D5830 works in top 'n tail mode with Class 37 37075 on 8 June 2014 as it approaches Oakworth (KWVR) with the 13:17 Oxenhope–Keighley service during the KWVR's annual diesel gala.

Class 31/4 31466 entered service as D5533 at Norwich depot in June 1959 and was withdrawn from Old Oak Common depot in February 2001. It entered preservation at the Dean Forest Railway (DFR) in March 2007 following lengthy storage but retained the maroon livery trialled by EWS before being withdrawn.

31466 pilots Class 31/1 31271 *Stratford 1840–2001* **as they curve through Townsend Fold (ELR) on 5 July 2014 whilst working the 15:26 Rawtenstall–Heywood service during the ELR's annual diesel gala. Attached to the rear of the train, but out of sight, is Class 55 'Deltic' D9009** *Alycidon* **and failed Class 40 D335.**

Class 31/1 31108 entered service as D5526 at Stratford depot in April 1959 and was withdrawn from Immingham depot in September 1991. It was stored at Scunthorpe until entering preservation at the Midland Railway Centre (MRC) in 1995.

31108 curves into Haworth (KWVR) on 6 June 2008 with the 10:35 Oxenhope–Keighley service during the KWVR's annual diesel gala.

Class 31/5 31556 entered service as D5823 at Darnall depot in November 1961 and was withdrawn from Springs Branch depot in December 1995. It transferred to the East Lancashire Railway (ELR) to provide spares for Class 31/4 D5600/31179/31435; the remnants were finally cut up in January 2010.

Left: 31556 lies in the siding at Bury South (ELR) from where it supplied spares for the restoration of Class 31/4 D5600/31435.

Class 31/1 31271 entered service as D5801 at Stratford depot in June 1961 and was withdrawn from Toton depot in May 1997. It was bought for spares to restore Class 31/1 31108 and arrived at the Midland Railway Centre (MRC) in May 1998 where it was decided to restore it to working order.

Right: 31271 *Stratford 1840–2001* crosses the River Irwell at Summerseat (ELR) on 5 July 2014 whilst working the 11:34 Ramsbottom–Bury shuttle service during the ELR's annual diesel gala.

Class 31/1 31119 entered service as D5537 at Stratford depot in June 1959 and was withdrawn from Springs Branch depot in September 1995. It entered preservation and moved to a private site in Newton Heath, Manchester but subsequently moved to the Embsay & Bolton Abbey Railway (EBAR) in January 2006, where it is based as at December 2016.

Left: 31119 approaches Bolton Abbey (EBAR) on 29 October 2006 with the 11:25 Embsay–Bolton Abbey service.

2.3: Type 3 Designs

The Type 3 classification was not included in the original Pilot Scheme categories but the experience gained with the East Anglia-based Class 30s uprated to 1600 hp confirmed that there was a role for the 1500–1999 hp range of locomotives and a specification was published. This resulted in three designs being received and for which follow-on orders were placed once the initial orders had proved themselves.

2.3.1: Class 33 – Birmingham RC&W

Builder
Birmingham RC&W

Year Built
1960–1962

Engine
Sulzer 8LDA28A rated at 1550 hp @ 750 rpm

Transmission
Electric

BR Fleet Numbers
D6500–6597; TOPS = 33001–33065; 33101–33119; 33201–212

History: This design was geared to the requirement of the Southern Region (SR) of BR for a locomotive with Electric Train Heat (ETH) hence no steam heating equipment was needed and the extra space allowed for the larger 8LDA engine to be adopted. The initial specification required that some locomotives be suited for work over the narrower Hastings route hence the construction of twelve locomotives (D6586–97) to the narrower 'Hastings Gauge' although they were not restricted solely to those routes.

When the Bournemouth Electrification Scheme was approved, it included the conversion of nineteen locomotives with push-pull equipment to operate the Bournemouth–Weymouth leg powering the non-motorised 4-car 4-TC trainsets that were attached/detached from the main services at Bournemouth.

TOPS Classification: The introduction of TOPS in the late 1960s and its application to Fleet Operations from 1974 allowed the various sub-groups to be identified:

33.0 = D6500–6585 (TOPS = 33001–33065) Standard locomotive
33.1 = Random locomotives fitted with push-pull equipment (TOPS = 33101–33119)
33.2 = D6586–6597 (TOPS = 33201–33212) Hastings gauge.

33021 bears the name *Captain Charles* as it stables at Cheddleton platform (CVR) at the dawn of a frosty 8 December 2012.

Class 33/0 33021 entered service at Hither Green depot as D6539 in January 1961 and was withdrawn from Stewarts Lane depot in September 1996 whence it was sold into preservation. The new owner restored the locomotive and hired it to main line operators before selling it on. The locomotive passed through further owners until the current owner moved it to the Churnet Valley Railway (CVR) in October 2010 where it is based as at December 2016.

Left: Class 33/0 33021 Captain Charles approaches Cheddleton (CVR), working in top 'n tail mode with Polish Class TkH 0-6-0T 2944, whilst working the 14:35 Cauldon Lowe–Froghall service.

Class 33/1 33102 *Sophie* entered service as D6513 at Hither Green depot in June 1960 and was withdrawn from Eastleigh depot in November 1992. It entered preservation with the North Staffs Diesel Group (NSDG) who transferred it to the Churnet Valley Railway (CVR) in October 1993.

Right: 33102 *Sophie* approaches Threshing Barn Crossing (MCR) on 31 December 2014 whilst working the 13:50 Ipstones–Froghall service in top 'n tail mode with Polish Class TkH 0-6-0T 2944.

Class 33/0 33063 entered service as D6583 at Hither Green depot in January 1962 and was withdrawn from Stewarts Lane depot in February 1997. It entered preservation with the South East Loco Group (SELG) at the East Kent Railway (EKR); the loco was subsequently moved to the Spa Valley Railway (SVR) where it is based as at December 2016.

Left: 33063 *R.J. Mitchell* forms the rear of an Eridge–Tunbridge Wells West service, worked in top 'n tail mode with LMS *Jinty* 3F 0-6-0T 47493, as it departs from Eridge on 17 June 2011.

Class 33/1 33102 *Sophie* pilots Polish Class TkH 0-6-0T 2944 as they approach Consall (CVR) on 1 July 2014 with the 10:35 Cheddleton–Froghall ecs.

33103 *Swordfish* pilots Class 31/4 31466 on their approach to Haworth (KWVR) on 25 May 2012 with the 10:25 Oxenhope–Keighley service during the KWVR's annual diesel gala.

Class 33/1 33103 *Swordfish* entered service as D6514 at Hither Green depot in July 1960 and was withdrawn from Eastleigh depot in February 1997. It entered preservation with Cambrian Trains, initially restored for main line service, but re-entered preservation at the Swanage Railway (SR) in March 2009. It was subsequently transferred to the Midland Railway Centre (MRC) where it is based as at December 2016.

Class 33/1 33109 entered service as D6525 at Hither Green depot in October 1960 and was withdrawn from Eastleigh depot in February 1997. It entered preservation with the 71A Locomotive Group at the Mid-Hants Railway (MHR) but subsequent sales ended with a private sale in February 2007 and a consequent move to the East Lancashire Railway (ELR) where the locomotive is based as at December 2016.

Left: 33109 pilots Class 47 D1501 past Heaps Bridge (ELR) on 8 January 2011 as they power the 14:00 Rawtenstall–Heywood service out of Bury.

Class 33/2 33201 entered service as D6586 at Hither Green depot in February 1962 and was withdrawn from Stewarts Lane in October 1993. It entered preservation with the BRC Workgroup at the Midland Railway Centre (MRC) where it is based as at December 2016.

Right: 33201 crosses the River Irwell at Summerseat (ELR) on 3 July 2002 with the 10:10 Irwell Vale–Bury service during the ELR's annual diesel gala.

Left: 33201 enters Irwell Vale (ELR) on 7 July 2002 whilst working the 11:20 Bury–Irwell Vale service in top 'n tail mode with Class 45/0 45060 *Sherwood Forester* during the ELR's annual diesel gala.

2.3.2: Class 35 – Beyer Peacock (Hymek)

Builder
Beyer Peacock

Year Built
1961–1964

Engine
Maybach MD870 rated at 1700 hp @ 1500 rpm

Transmission
Hydraulic

BR Fleet Numbers
D7000–7100; TOPS = Class 35 (TOPS numbers never carried)

History: This design was geared to the requirements of the Western Region (WR) of BR and was designed to be the replacement for the 'Grange', 'Hall' and 'Manor' classes of mixed traffic 4-6-0 locomotives. The WR had identified a need for 300 Type 3 locomotives to replace steam traction in South Wales but the superior braking performance of the Class 37 design saw the additional order for 200 locomotives be placed with English Electric. Whilst essentially a competent locomotive design, considered superior to the Class 37 design, it was condemned with all locomotives using hydraulic transmission under the 1968 Traction Plan when electric transmission was adopted as the future standard.

TOPS Classification: The introduction of TOPS in the late 1960s and its application to Fleet Operations from 1974 saw the fleet allocated Class 35 but no class member ever carried a TOPS number.

D7076 entered service at Old Oak Common depot in May 1963 and was withdrawn from Bristol Bath Road depot in May 1973. Following a short period in store it was transferred to Departmental duties with the Railway Technical Centre at Derby between August 1974–November 1982. When withdrawn from Departmental service it entered preservation with the East Lancashire Railway (ELR) in early 1983.

Left: D7076 makes a typically smoky departure from Irwell Vale (ELR) on 4 July 2015 with the 11:47 Heywood–Rawtenstall service during the ELR's annual diesel gala.

Right: D7076 curves through Townsend Fold (ELR) on 9 July 2005 with the 15:40 Rawtenstall–Heywood service during the ELR's annual diesel gala.

D7017 entered service at Bristol Bath Road depot in January 1962 and was withdrawn from Old Oak Common depot in March 1975. It entered preservation with the Diesel & Electric Preservation Group and moved to Taunton in July 1975 before transferring to the West Somerset Railway in March 1976 where it is based as at December 2016.

Note of interest
1. D7017 was the first diesel locomotive to be preserved by public subscription thus pointing the way forward for future diesel/electric preservation schemes.

Left: D7017 rests in the Williton (WSR) base of the Diesel & Electric Group on 20 March 2011.

Above: D7076 accelerates the 12:11 Kidderminster–Bridgnorth service through Hayes Bridge (SVR) on 2 October 2015 during the SVR's annual diesel gala.

Left: D7076 pilots Class 33/1 33109 *Captain Bill Smith RN* through Burrs (ELR) on 6 March 2010 whilst working the 12:05 Heywood–Rawtenstall service during the ELR's Spring diesel gala.

2.3.3: Class 37 – English Electric Company

Builder
English Electric (Vulcan Foundry); English Electric (Robert Stephenson Hawthorn (RSH) Darlington)

Year Built
1960–1965

Engine
English Electric 12CSVT rated at 1750 hp @ 850 rpm

Transmission
Electric

BR Fleet Numbers
D6600–6608; D6700–6999; TOPS = 37001–37308
See also TOPS notes below

History: The initial order for this design (D6700–29) was allocated to East Anglia where the uprated Class 31s had identified the value of the Type 3 range for mixed traffic duties and further orders were placed for duties in coal mining areas where the 6-axle locomotive proved suitable for working the unfitted coal trains then being operated. A pair of locomotives were trialled in South Wales leading to further orders (D6819–6999; D6600–6608) being placed to eliminate steam traction from South Wales in preference to the WR's hope of placing further Class 35 orders.

In the 1980s the initial demand for a replacement Type 3 design was cancelled and a number of Class 37s were modified instead to create new sub-groups with the aim of operating the refurbished locomotives for a further twenty years. These new classes are identified as under.

Notes of interest
1. Withdrawal dates of class members are confused due to:-
    a. stored locomotives transferred to HQ (Headquarters) from where locomotives suffered component recovery
    b. locomotives transferred to HQ (Headquarters) for special duties such as hire to French operators
    c. locomotives' official withdrawal dates being after purchase date by individuals/ companies

2. The question of preservation becomes confused when some purchasers sought to use them for main line duty but maintained/operated them on heritage lines when not contracted to main line operations.
3. In 2014 both Colas Railfreight and Direct Rail Services (DRS) identified a need for Class 37 locomotives but their only source was preserved locomotives; both companies bought or hired preserved locomotives for return to main line duties – and out of preservation.

TOPS Classification: The introduction of TOPS in the late 1960s and its application to Fleet Operations from 1974 allowed various sub-groups to be identified:

37.0 = D6600–6608; D6700–6999; TOPS = 37001–308

Sub-groups created for specific purposes in the 1980s:

37.3 = 37310–37314 (split headcode) + 37320–37326 (4-character headcode) for Hunterston steel traffic
37330–37335 (split headcode) + 37340–37345 (4-character headcode) with CP7 bogies for Sandite duties
37350–37359 (split headcode) + 37370–37384 (4-character headcode) with CP7 bogies for Departmental duties
37.4 = 37401–37431 with ETH for secondary passenger duties
37.5 = 37501–521 for Steel Sector duties
37667–37699 for Railfreight duties
37.6 = 37601–37612 for Eurostar duties (later cancelled) and subsequently bought by Direct Rail Services (DRS)
37.7 = 37701–37899 (with gaps) for Coal and Steel Sector duties
37.9 = 37901–37904 with Mirrlees MB275T rated at 1800 hp @ 1000 rpm;
37905–37906 with Ruston RK270T rated at 1800 hp @ 900 rpm;
both Class 37/9 sub-groups were allocated to Steel Sector based at Cardiff to compare engine performance
97.3 = 97301–97304 with ETRMS for Cambrian Line services

Class 37/0 D6700 entered service at Stratford depot in December 1960 and was withdrawn from Toton depot in December 1999. Following a period of storage at Thornaby depot, it entered preservation with the National Rail Museum (NRM) at York in August 2000.

Above: D6700 *NRM National Rail Museum* forms the rear of the 13:05 Bury–Irwell Vale service at Ramsbottom (ELR) on 7 July 2002 during the ELR's annual diesel gala.

Top Right: D6700 *NRM National Rail Museum* powers away from Barrow Hill (BHR) platform on 28 November 2005 whilst hauling the site's branch shuttle.

Bottom Right: D6700 stands at Grosmont (NYMR) on 9 September 2009 whilst powering a Grosmont–Pickering charter for Railway Safety Executive staff.

Class 37/0 37109 entered traffic as D6809 at Darnall depot in February 1963 and was withdrawn from Headquarters stock in August 2007. It entered preservation at the East Lancashire Railway (ELR) in November 2007.

Left: 37109 bears faded EWS livery as it curves past Townsend Fold (ELR) on 3 July 2008 with the 15:40 Rawtenstall–Heywood service during the ELR's annual diesel gala.

Bottom Left: 37109 pilots Class 33/1 D6525/33109 *Captain Bill Smith RN* on 6 March 2010 as they depart from Ramsbottom (ELR) with the 09:20 Bury–Rawtenstall service.

Class 37/0 37075 entered service as D6775 at Thornaby depot in September 1962 and from where it was withdrawn in November 1999 following storage since August 1994. It was purchased for preservation in August 1999 and entered preservation at the Great Central Railway (North) (GCRN) since when it has passed through further sales until arriving at the Keighley & Worth Valley Railway (KWVR) in March 2012, where it is based as at December 2016.

Bottom Right: 37075 pilots Class 20 20031 as they approach Haworth (KWVR) on 25 May 2012 with the 09:40 Oxenhope–Keighley service.

6940 runs alongside the River Dee as it departs from Glyndyfrdwy (LR) on 2 October 2010 with the 16:15 Llangollen Goods Jn–Carrog Demonstration Freight during an LR Diesel Running Day.

Class 37/0 6940/37240 entered service as D6940 at Worcester depot in August 1964 and was withdrawn from Crewe Diesel depot in December 1999 whence it entered preservation in July 2002 with the Llangollen Railway (LR).

Class 37/0 37197 entered service as D6897 at Landore depot in April 1964 and was withdrawn from Headquarters stock in December 1999 followed by sale to Ian Riley Engineering. It was originally intended as support for main line steam operations but 37197 was sold to the West Coast Railway Company (WCRC) in May 2004 and subsequently to Direct Rail Services (DRS) in June 2006.

Left: 37197 forms the rear of the 14:00 Rawtenstall–Bury service on 17 November 2001 as it calls at Ramsbottom (ELR) during its 'shakedown' trials.

Class 37/0 37294 entered service as D6994 at Cardiff Canton depot in July 1965 and was withdrawn from Toton depot in May 2007 whence it entered preservation with the Embsay & Bolton Abbey Railway (EBAR) in March 2009.

Right: 37294 drifts down the gradient at Hambleton (EBAR) on 25 July 2010 whilst working the 14:30 Embsay–Bolton Abbey service during a Diesel Running Day.

Class 37/0 37190 entered service as D6890 at Landore depot in January 1964 and was withdrawn from Canton depot in July 1992 from where it was moved to Gateshead for storage; it entered preservation with the Midland Railway Centre (MRC) during 1995.

Left: 37190 pilots Class 50 50007 *Sir Edward Elgar* as they depart from Oxenhope (KWVR) with the 14:30 Oxenhope–Keighley service on 3 August 2002 during a KWVR diesel gala.

Class 37/0 37175 entered service as D6875 at Cardiff Canton depot in September 1963 and was withdrawn from Toton depot in December 1999. It entered Departmental service that included joining the Heritage Fleet and entered preservation with the Weardale Railway (WR) in July 2006. It then moved to the Bo'ness & Kinneil Railway (BKR) from where it was purchased by Colas Railfreight during 2015 hence returning to main line service – and out of preservation.

Left: 37175 basks in the sunshine outside Bo'ness depot (BKR) on 23 February 2009 shortly after completion of its restoration.

Class 37/0 37275 entered traffic as D6975 at Cardiff Canton depot in April 1965 and was withdrawn from Headquarters stock in March 2000. After a lengthy period in store it entered preservation at the Weardale Railway (WR) in July 2004 but following further transfers it is based at the South Devon Railway (SDR) as at December 2016.

Right: 37275 draws its trainset out of Ramsbottom (ELR) on 6 July 2012 as it moves to the sidings after its arrival with a Bury–Ramsbottom shuttle service during the ELR's annual diesel gala.

Class 37/5 37515 entered service as D6764 at Thornaby depot in November 1962 and was withdrawn from Headquarters stock in June 1999. It entered Departmental service, including being hired to French contractors between June 1999 and October 2000, and was finally withdrawn from service in January 2003. It was bought by Harry Needle for spot hire but offered to heritage lines when not under contract. Following a collision at Barrow Hill (BHR) in January 2008 the locomotive was stored until transfer for scrap to TJ Thomson at Stockton in July 2010.

Left: 37515 displays an early Harry Needle Railway Company (HNRC) livery at Barrow Hill (BHR) on 28 November 2005 during a diesel gala event.

Class 37/4 37403 entered service as D6607 at Landore depot in October 1965 and was withdrawn from Headquarters stock in September 2002 to enter storage. Although purchased in November 2007, it was January 2009 when the locomotive entered preservation at the Bo'ness & Kinneil Railway (BKR) for a restoration that was completed during 2016 by Direct Rail Services (DRS) following a hiring agreement it made to supplement its Class 37/4 fleet.

Left: 37403 stands outside Bo'ness shed (BKR) on 23 February 2009 awaiting its turn in the restoration queue.

Right: Class 37/0 37240 growls away from Glyndyfrdwy (LR) on 7 October 2006 with the 13:00 Llangollen–Carrog service during an LR Diesel Running Day.

Class 37/0 37261 entered service as D6961 at Tinsley depot in January 1965 and was withdrawn from Headquarters stock in July 1999 from where it was contracted to French infrastructure contracts between August 1999 and July 2000. Following a lengthy period in store it was sold to Ian Riley Engineering in 2001; it was originally intended as support for main line steam operations but 37261 was sold to the West Coast Railway Company (WCRC) in May 2004 and subsequently to Direct Rail Services (DRS) in November 2005. It was withdrawn from service in 2015 and in July 2015 was moved to the Bo'ness base of the Scottish Class 37 Group where it is being restored to working order as of December 2016.

Left: 37261 undergoes overhaul in Ian Riley's workshops on the ELR on 19 January 2002.

Left: Class 37/0 37197 pilots Class 40 40135 through Burrs (ELR) as they power the 18:00 Bury–Rawtenstall service on 5 July 2003 during the ELR's annual diesel gala.

Class 37/4 37424 entered service as D6979 at Cardiff Canton depot in May 1965 and was withdrawn from Toton depot in June 2008. It entered preservation at the Churnet Valley Railway (CVR) in 2008 but whilst awaiting restoration it was bought by Direct Rail Services (DRS) during 2015 as the company sought to supplement its Class 37/4 fleet.

Right: 37424 awaits restoration at the Cheddleton (CVR) on 6 June 2012 with sister locomotive 37407 which subsequently joined 37424 in the purchase by DRS.

Class 37/4 37418 entered service as D6971 at Cardiff Canton depot in March 1965 and was withdrawn from Toton depot in February 2007, although not withdrawn from stock until February 2008. It entered preservation with the East Lancashire Railway (ELR) in March 2009.

Left: 37418 *Pectinidae* is pilotted by Class 55 'Deltic' 55022 *Royal Scots Grey* out of Irwell Vale (ELR) on 9 January 2010 whilst working the 11:30 Rawtenstall–Heywood service.

A rare Class 37/9 pairing in preservation sees 37906 pilot 37901 *Mirrlees Pioneer* past Townsend Fold (ELR) on 3 July 2008 whilst working the 16:30 Rawtenstall–Heywood service during the ELR's annual diesel gala.

Class 37/9 37906 entered service as D6906 at Landore depot in November 1963 and was withdrawn from Headquarters stock for spares recovery in January 1999. It was bought in June 2006, although not officially withdrawn from stock until August 2006, and entered preservation at the Severn Valley Railway (SVR) in August 2006. Subsequent transfers have resulted in it being bought for main line service in 2016 with UK Rail Leasings (UKRL).

Right: 37906 powers out of Irwell Vale (ELR) on 3 July 2008 with the 11:30 Rawtenstall–Heywood service during the ELR's annual diesel gala.

Class 37/9 37901 entered service as D6850 at Cardiff Canton depot in July 1963 and was withdrawn from Headquarters stock in December 1999. After lengthy storage it entered preservation at the Llangollen Railway (LR) in October 2003 but subsequent transfers have resulted in it being bought for main line service in 2016 with Colas Railfreight.

Below Left: 37901 *Mirrlees Pioneer* passes Fisherman's Crossing on 6 October 2007 as it nears Glyndyfrdwy (LR) with the 16:20 Carrog–Llangollen Goods Jn service during an LR Diesel Running Day.

Below Right: 37901 *Mirrlees Pioneer* works in top 'n tail mode with Class 73/1 73101 *The Royal Alex* as they approach Carrog (LR) on 11 April 2008 with the 10:00 Llangollen–Carrog service during an LR Diesel Running Day.

2.4: Type 4 Designs

The Type 4 (Pilot Scheme Type C) designs were specified as the express passenger locomotive with 2000 hp considered as the maximum power that would be required. As the new designs were being delivered BR became aware that increased loads and speeds were outpacing their ability to meet the schedules. This gave rise to the 2nd generation of designs with engines rated at 2750 hp and above.

In practice the early Type 4 designs proved extremely robust and, apart from those designs with hydraulic transmission, they provided over 25 years' service with many only being withdrawn as traffic patterns changed in the 1970s/1980s. By this time, however, the ethos of diesel locomotive preservation had gained greater acceptance leading to the preservation of examples of most classes.

2.4.1: Class 40 – English Electric

Builder
English Electric (Vulcan); English Electric (Robert Stephenson Hawthorn (RSH) Darlington)

Year Built
1958–1962

Engine
English Electric 16-cylinder 16SVT Mk II rated at 2000 hp @ 850 rpm

Transmission
Electric

BR Fleet Numbers
D200–399; TOPS = 40001–199

History: This Pilot Scheme design of ten locomotives (D200–209) was based on the profile of the LMSR Derby Twins (10000/1) with the bogie design of the SR Trio (10201–3) and proved sufficiently successful that follow-up orders were placed for a further 190 examples. Their demise came in the 1980s but seven examples have been preserved, including class doyen D200 in the National Rail Museum collection.

D213 entered service at Willesden depot in June 1959 and was withdrawn from Longsight depot in January 1985 but was retained as BR's 'exhibit' locomotive until February 1988 when it was stored at Crewe. It was bought privately from the May 1988 Tender list and, following asbestos removal, entered preservation with the South Yorkshire Railway (SYR) at Meadowhall during 1989. D213 moved to the Midland Railway Centre (MRC) in September 1999 then to Barrow Hill (BHR) in January 2003 for restoration; with the owner's death in October 2011 the work was continued by staff from Harry Needle Railway Company (HNRC) and the locomotive remains at Barrow Hill (BHR) as at December 2016.

D213 *Andania* is displayed under the night lights at Barrow Hill (BHR) on 23 September 2015 during a weekend gala event.

40135 entered service as D335 at Crewe depot in March 1961 and was withdrawn from Longsight depot in January 1985 from where it was transferred to Departmental stock until withdrawal in December 1986. It was stored until entering preservation by the Class 40 Preservation Society (CFPS) at the East Lancashire Railway (ELR) in May 1988.

Right: D335 drifts down Broadfield bank on 13 September 2003 whilst working the 15:03 Heywood–Bury service in top 'n tail mode with sister locomotive 40145.

Below: D335 draws to a halt at Irwell Vale (ELR) on 11 November 2006 whilst working the 13:45 Bury–Rawtenstall service in top 'n tail mode with sister locomotive 40145.

40106 entered service as D306 at Crewe depot in October 1960 and was withdrawn from Longsight depot in April 1983. It entered preservation by a private owner at the Great Central Railway (GCR) in August 1984; it was bought by the Class 40 Preservation Society (CFPS) in November 2015 and moved to the CFPS base at the East Lancashire Railway (ELR) during 2016.

Left: 40106 *Atlantic Conveyor* climbs past Northwood Lane (SVR) on 3 October 2014 with the 12:54 Bridgnorth–Kidderminster service during the SVR's annual diesel gala.

Below: Earlier in the day 40106 *Atlantic Conveyor* shunts a trainset at Kidderminster (SVR) prior to working a service to Bridgnorth.

40145 entered service as D345 at Leeds Neville Hill depot in May 1961 and was withdrawn from Longsight depot in June 1983. It entered preservation by the Class 40 Preservation Society (CFPS) at the East Lancashire Railway (ELR) in February 1984 thus becoming the first member of its class to be preserved.

Displaying the variety of liveries operated by BR:

Right: 40145 displays the large logo livery at Ramsbottom (ELR) on 6 March 2010 as it hauls a stock move from the sidings to the station prior to working a Ramsbottom–Bury shuttle service.

Below Left: D345 carries its original livery at Bury (ELR) on 4 July 2002 when stabled at the platform during the ELR's annual diesel gala.

Below Right: 40145 carries the corporate blue livery as it passes Burrs (ELR) on 7 July 2007 with the 13:20 Heywood–Rawtenstall service during the ELR's annual diesel gala.

2.4.2: *Class 42 – BR Swindon*

Builder
BR Swindon

Year Built
1958–1961

Engine
2 x Maybach MD650 rated at 1152 hp @ 1530 rpm (see note below)

Transmission
Hydraulic

BR Fleet Numbers
D800–832; D866–870; TOPS = Class 42 (TOPS numbers never carried)

History: This design was not initially part of the Pilot Scheme but the Western Region of BR sought to trial the advantages of the German V200 design hence authority was gained to build three prototype locomotives (D800–802) at Swindon Works using MD650 engines rated at 1056 hp @ 1400 rpm, built under licence by Bristol-Siddeley, and include them in the Pilot Scheme. The WR placed a follow-up order for thirty-five locomotives with the 1152 hp engines, also built under licence by Bristol-Siddeley, but their life was shortened by the National Traction Plan in 1968 which approved the withdrawal of all locomotive designs with hydraulic transmission despite the fleet being designated TOPS Class 42.

Notes of Interest

1. For political reasons a 2nd batch of thirty-three locomotives (D833–865) was ordered from North British Locomotive Company (NBL) but these were fitted with MAN engines, built under licence by NBL, and proved less reliable in service. Although designated Class 43 under TOPS, this class was also slated for withdrawal under the 1968 National Traction Plan and none survived to be preserved.
2. When D821 *Greyhound* was preserved by the nascent Diesel Traction Group (DTG) it was both the first main line diesel to be preserved and the first to be funded from private sources.

D832 *Onslaught* entered service at Laira depot in February 1961 and was withdrawn from there in December 1972 whence it was transferred to Derby Research Centre until being withdrawn in June 1979. It was bought privately and, following display at Horwich Works Open Day in August 1980, it entered preservation at the East Lancashire Railway (ELR).

D832 *Onslaught* pilots Class 52 D1015 *Western Champion* past Ewood (ELR) on 5 July 2007 whilst working the 11:15 Heywood–Rawtenstall service during the ELR's annual diesel gala.

D821 *Greyhound* **approaches Highley (SVR) on 8 October 2009 with the 14:40 Kidderminster–Highley service.**

D821 *Greyhound* entered service at Laira depot in May 1960 from where it was withdrawn in December 1972 and stored until May 1973 when it was bought by the nascent Diesel Traction Group (DTG). It entered preservation at the Didcot Railway Centre but made further moves until September 1991 when it became based at the Severn Valley Railway (SVR) with other DTG locomotives.

2.4.3: *Classes 44 thru 46 – BR Workshops*

Builder
BR Crewe; BR Derby

Year Built
1960–1963

Engine
Sulzer 12LDA28B rated at 2500 hp @ 750 rpm (see note below)

Transmission
Electric

BR Fleet Numbers
D1–10 (TOPS = 44001–44010); D11–137 (TOPS = 45001–45077; 45101–45150); D138–193 (TOPS = 46001–46056)

History: The Pilot Scheme design (D1–10) was similar to that of the Class 40 but Derby Works elected to adopt the Sulzer 12LDA28 engine rated at 2300 hp @ 750 rpm when English Electric tendered its (Class 40) design. When the first follow-on order was placed the engine had been uprated to the 2500 hp specification and this was adopted for both the Class 45 and 46 variants. The electrical equipment was supplied by Crompton Parkinson but when deliveries became subject to delays BR turned to Brush Traction as an alternative supplier for the final batch that was subsequently designated TOPS Class 46.

TOPS Classification: The introduction of TOPS in the late 1960s and its application to Fleet Operations from 1974 allowed the three classes, whilst similar in external features, to be separately identified:

44.0 = D1–10 Original Pilot Scheme locomotives with disc indicators
45.0 = D11–137 with Crompton Parkinson electrical equipment; D11–31 + D68–107 with split headcode and D32–67 + D108–137 with 4-character headcode
    As TOPS numbering was being applied, 50 locomotives were selected in random order for fitting with Electrical Train Heat (ETH) equipment resulting in:-
45.0 = locomotives with either steam heat or no heat (following removal)
45.1 = locomotives with Electric Train Heat (ETH)
46.0 = locomotives with Brush electrical equipment

Class 45/0 45060 *Sherwood Forester* entered service as D100 at Derby depot in May 1961 and was withdrawn from Toton depot in December 1985. It was stored until being bought by the Pioneer Loco Group in January 1987 and entered preservation at Peak Rail (PR) later that year. Following further changes of location it is based at Barrow Hill (BHR) as at December 2016.

45060 Sherwood Forester pilots Class 45/1 45135 3rd Carabinier on 6 July 2002 as they arrive at Irwell Vale (ELR) with the 10:45 Bury–Irwell Vale service being worked in top 'n tail mode with Class 33/2 33201 during the ELR's annual diesel gala.

Class 45/1 45112 *The Royal Army Ordnance Corps* entered service as D61 at Derby depot in March 1962 and was withdrawn from Tinsley depot in May 1987. It was bought privately for main line use and, as at June 2016, is owned by Nemesis Rail based at Burton on Trent.

Left: 45112 *The Royal Army Ordnance Corps* is stabled in the sidings of Harry Needle Railway Company (HNRC) at Barrow Hill (BHR) on 22 August 2008.

Class 45/1 45105 entered service as D86 at Derby depot in March 1961 and was withdrawn from Tinsley depot in May 1987 whence it was bought by the Pioneer Loco Group and, as at December 2016, was under restoration at Barrow Hill Roundhouse (BHR).

Right: 45105 stabled within the Barrow Hill Roundhouse on 22 August 2008 whilst undergoing restoration to working order.

Class 45/1 45135 *3rd Carabinier* entered service as D99 at Derby depot in May 1961 and was withdrawn from Tinsley depot in May 1987. It was bought by the Pioneer Loco Group and entered preservation at the Peak Rail (PR) site located at Matlock but subsequently moved to the East Lancashire Railway (ELR) in June 1999, where it is based as at December 2016.

Left: 45135 *3rd Carabinier* eases out of Rawtenstall (ELR) on 16 March 2002 with the 17:00 Rawtenstall–Bury service.

Class 46 46010 entered service as D147 at Derby depot in December 1961 but was immediately 'loaned' to Corkerhill depot for crew/artisan training and was withdrawn from Gateshead depot in November 1984 whence it was transferred to Doncaster for storage. It was bought by the Llangollen Diesel Group (LDG) in February 1993 and entered preservation at the Llangollen Railway (LR). It was subsequently sold to the Western Peak Group (WPG) who transferred it to Great Central Railway (North) (GCRN) during 2012, where it is based as at December 2016.

Opposite Page: 46010 approaches Fishermen's Crossing (LR) on 6 October 2007 as it nears Glyndyfrdwy with the 13:50 Carrog–Llangollen service.

This Page

Class 46 46035 entered service as D172 at Gateshead depot in July 1962 and was withdrawn from there in November 1984 whence it entered Departmental service at the Derby Research Centre until final withdrawal in January 1991. It was bought by Pete Waterman and overhauled for main line service but as at December 2016 it is in long-term store at the Rowsley base of Peak Rail (PR) awaiting a decision regarding its future.

Right: 46035 forms the rear of the 16:00 Rawtenstall–Bury service when seen at Ramsbottom (ELR) on 16 March 2002.

Below: 45060 *Sherwood Forester* awaits departure from Summerseat (ELR) on 2 July 2010 whilst working the 13:36 Rawtenstall–Heywood service during the ELR's annual diesel gala.

2.4.4: Class 47 – Brush Traction

Builder
Brush Traction; BR Crewe

Year Built
1962–1967

Engine
Sulzer 12LDA28C rated at 2580 hp @ 750 rpm (see note below)

Transmission
Electric

BR Fleet Numbers
D1100–1111; D1500–1999; TOPS = See note below

History: An early result of operating the 1st Generation of diesel locomotives was the realisation that express passenger services required a locomotive in the power range of 2750 hp or greater and a specification was issued by BR. This led to a trio of designs but the financial stability of Brush Traction and its willingness to meet BR demands (including BR construction of part of any order) saw its design gain approval as the 'standard' Type 4 locomotive.

A first order for 20 locomotives (D1500–1519) quickly led to follow-on orders for a total of 512 locomotives with construction shared between Brush Traction (310 locomotives) and BR Crewe (202 locomotives). With technical changes such as fitting of slow-speed equipment, freight dedicated locomotives without heating equipment and the retrospective fitting of air brake equipment and ETH to random locomotives, uniformity was quickly lost and even with the introduction of TOPS classifications, variety became a common factor even within classes.

An early problem, however, was the appearance of major faults in the Sulzer engine which were resolved by the de-rating of the output to 2580 hp plus engine modifications that were applied as the problems appeared. Despite this the design has proved a workhorse to train operators and as at December 2016 many examples still operate main line duties whilst further examples are preserved on heritage lines.

TOPS Classification: The introduction of TOPS in the late 1960s and its application to Fleet Operations from 1974 allowed the various sub-groups, whilst similar in external features, to be separately identified:

47.0 = 47001–47299 locomotives with steam or no heat; some examples have Slow Speed Equipment for MGR duties

47.3 = 47300–47381 locomotives designed for freight duties

47.4 = D1500–1519 (47401–47420) are the original locomotives fitted with electric train heating equipment from new
47421–47600; 47602–47665 retrospectively fitted with improved ETH equipment
47671–47677 regeared for Highland Line/Sleeper duties

47.6 = 47601-test bed locomotive for Class 56

47.7 = 47701–47716 converted for Edinburgh-Glasgow (later ScotRail) push-pull services
47721–47793 converted for Rail Express Systems (RES) duties including charter services
47798–47799 dedicated to Royal Train duties with security equipment fitted

47.8 = 47801–47854 refurbished Class 47/4 and 47/7 (RES) locomotives with increased fuel capacity for long range duties

47.9 = 47901-test bed locomotive for Class 58
47971–47976 locomotives transferred to Departmental duties

48.0 = D1702–1706 fitted with Sulzer 12LVA24 engine rated at 2650 hp @ 1050 rpm from new but restored to Class 47/0 specification in the early 1970s.

Class (47/4) Doyen 47401 entered traffic as D1500 at Finsbury Park depot in September 1962 and was withdrawn from Immingham depot in June 1992. It was bought by the 47401 Project and entered preservation at the Midland Railway Centre (MRC) in July 1993, where it is based as at December 2016.

Opposite: 47401 *North Eastern* heads a line of stabled preserved locomotives at the Swanwick base of the MRC on 8 November 2014.

Class 47/0 47292 entered service as D1994 at York depot in April 1966 and was withdrawn from service by Freightliner in December 2003. It was sold by tender to a private individual and entered preservation at the Great Central Railway (North) (GCRN) in June 2007, where it is based as at December 2016.

Left: 47292 powers away from Ramsbottom (ELR) on 4 July 2009 whilst working the 10:25 Heywood–Rawtenstall service during the ELR's annual diesel gala.

Class 47/3 47376 entered service as D1895 at Tinsley depot in September 1965 and was withdrawn from service by Freightliner in June 2001. It was bought by the Brush Type 4 Fund and entered preservation at the Gloucestershire Warwickshire Railway (GWR) in November 2002, where it is based as at December 2016.

Right (Image 149): 47376 *Freightliner 1995* forms the rear of the 15:30 Toddington–Gotherington service as it leaves Toddington (GWR) behind 'Hall' Class 4-6-0 7903 *Foremarke Hall* on 23 October 2010.

Class 47/3 47367 entered service as D1886 at Immingham depot in August 1965 and was withdrawn from service by Freightliner in January 2001. It was bought by the Stratford 47 Group and entered preservation at the North Norfolk Railway (NNR) in February 2003 but subsequently moved to the Mid-Norfolk Railway (MNR) where it is based as at December 2016.

Left: 47367 stands in Sheringham yard (NNR) on 16 August 2004 undergoing restoration to working order.

Class 47/4 D1501 entered service at Finsbury Park depot in November 1962 and was withdrawn from Immingham depot in July 1992. It was bought by Pete Waterman and entered preservation at the East Lancashire Railway (ELR) in December 1993, where it is based as at December 2016.

Scenes of D1501 at work on the ELR includes:

Right: passing Townsend Fold on the approach to Rawtenstall on 6 March 2010 whilst working the 09:35 Heywood–Rawtenstall service.

Below Left: approaching Ramsbottom on 5 July 2014 whilst working the 10:06 Rawtenstall–Heywood service during the ELR's annual diesel gala.

Below Right: passing Heaps Bridge on 8 January 2011 whilst working the 15:20 Heywood–Rawtenstall service.

Class 47/4 47596 entered service as D1933 at Bristol Bath Rd depot in March 1966 and was withdrawn from Crewe depot in November 2002. It was bought by the Stratford 47 Group in March 2003 and entered preservation at Tyseley Locomotive Works (TLW) before moving to its current base, as at December 2016, with the Mid-Norfolk Railway (MNR) in November 2006.

Left: **47596** *Aldeburgh Festival***, working in top 'n tail mode with Class 47 D1501, eases the stock of a Bury–Ramsbottom service into Ramsbottom sidings on 5 July 2013 during the ELR's annual diesel gala.**

Class 47/4 D1566 entered service at Tinsley depot in March 1964 and was withdrawn from service at Stratford depot in May 1993. It was bought by the Llangollen Diesel Group (LDG) and entered preservation at the Llangollen Railway (LR) in December 1996, where it is based as at December 2016.

Below: **D1566** *Orion* **descends from the Dee Bridge (LR) as it approaches Llangollen on 7 October 2006 with the 15:50 Carrog–Llangollen service.**

Class 47/4 47643 entered service as D1970 at Haymarket depot in October 1965 and was withdrawn from Inverness depot in April 1992. It was bought by the Scottish Railways Preservation Society (SRPS) Diesel Group and entered preservation at the Bo'ness & Kinneil Railway (BKR) in October 1995, where it is based as at December 2016.

Right: 47643 curves past Townsend Fold (ELR) on 4 July 2015 as it approaches Rawtenstall with the 14:51 Heywood–Rawtenstall service during the ELR's annual diesel gala.

Class 47/4 47579 entered service as D1778 at Tinsley depot in October 1964 and was withdrawn from Toton depot in February 2004. It was bought by John Jolly, the owner of Mangapps Farm, in March 2007 and entered preservation at Mangapps Farm in April 2007.

Below Left: 47579 *James Nightall GC* crosses the River Irwell after leaving Summerseat (ELR) on 5 July 2013 with the 10:25 Heywood–Rawtenstall service during the ELR's annual diesel gala.

Class 47/4 47580 entered service as D1762 at Tinsley depot in September 1964 and was withdrawn from Toton depot in February 2004. It was bought by the Stratford 47 Group in March 2007 and entered preservation at Tyseley Locomotive Works (TLW) in April 2007 before moving to the Mid-Norfolk Railway (MNR) where it is based as at December 2016.

Below Right: 47580 *County of Essex* crosses the River Irwell after leaving Summerseat (ELR) on 5 July 2014 with the 11:15 Heywood–Rawtenstall service during the ELR's annual diesel gala.

Class 47/4 47524 entered service as D1107 at York depot in January 1967 and was withdrawn from Crewe depot in November 2002. It was bought by the North Staffs Diesel Group (NSDG) in February 2002 and entered preservation at the Churnet Valley Railway (CVR) in October 2005 where it is based as at December 2016.

Left: 47524 stands in Cheddleton yard (CVR) on 14 August 2014 whilst awaiting the start of its restoration.

Class 47/0 D1705 entered service as a Class 48 locomotive at Darnall depot in November 1965 and was withdrawn from Tinsley depot in July 1994. Initially bought by Pete Waterman, it entered preservation at the East Lancashire Railway (ELR) but was subsequently sold to the Type 1 Loco Group which moved the locomotive to the Great Central Railway (GCR) in December 1996, where it is based as at December 2016.

Right: D1705 *Sparrow Hawk* stands in Quorn yard (GCR) on 25 April 2013 having served as a display item during a recent gala event.

Class 47/0 D1524 entered service at Finsbury Park depot in June 1963 and was withdrawn from Bescot depot in December 1998 whence it transferred to the EWS Heritage Fleet. When finally withdrawn from Old Oak Common depot it was purchased privately and entered preservation at the Embsay & Bolton Abbey Railway (EBAR) in June 2006.

Left: D1524 pilots Class 31 31119 out of Embsay (EBAR) on 29 October 2006 as they depart with the 09:30 Embsay–Bolton Abbey service.

Class 47/7 47701 entered service as D1932 at Bristol Bath Rd depot in March 1966 and was withdrawn from Crewe depot during 1996. It was bought by Pete Waterman who sold it on to Tracy Lear during 1997 who then hired it to Fragonset for spot-hire duties. It was withdrawn from main line service in December 2003 and was stored until February 2007 when a successful overhaul saw it attending the Gloucestershire Warwickshire Railway (GWR) gala event then move to the Dartmoor Railway (DR) during the year.

A dispute between the DR and the locomotive owner saw the locomotive placed in store and subsequent negotiations saw the locomotive leave preservation when bought by Nemesis Rail in October 2014 for possible main line duties.

Left: 47701 *Waverley* stands in Barrow Hill (BHR) sidings on 5 October 2003 as a display item during a BHR gala event.

Class 47/7 47798 entered service as D1656 at Landore depot and was withdrawn from EWS stock in February 2004, having been a dedicated 'Royal Train' locomotive since May 1995. It entered preservation with the National Rail Museum (NRM) in August 2004 and as at December 2016 is used as an exhibit at many diesel gala events.

Right: 47798 *Prince William* takes a break from Royal duty on 7 October 2001 as it provides an event exhibit at Barrow Hill (BHR) during a diesel gala event.

Class 47/7 47785 entered service as D1909 at Cardiff Canton depot in November 1965 and was withdrawn from Crewe depot in September 2003. It was bought privately and entered preservation with the Stainmore Railway (SR), based at Kirkby Stephen, in July 2007 but was subsequently moved to the Wensleydale Railway (WR) during 2015, where it is based as at December 2016.

Left: 47785 stands at Kirkby Stephen East's platform (SR) on 28 January 2012 whilst awaiting the start of its restoration.

2.4.5: Class 50 – English Electric

Builder
English Electric (Vulcan)

Year Built
1967–1968

Engine
English Electric 16-cylinder 16CSVT rated at 2700 hp @ 850 rpm

Transmission
Electric

BR Fleet Numbers
D400–449; TOPS = 50001–50050

50035 entered service as D435 with D05 (Stoke Division) in August 1968 and was withdrawn from Laira depot in August 1990. It was officially handed over to the Fifty Fund at the Old Oak Common Open Day in 1991 and entered preservation at St Leonards depot where restoration began. It moved to the Severn Valley Railway (SVR) in September 2006, where it is based as at December 2016.

50044 entered service as D444 with D05 (Stoke Division) in November 1968 and was withdrawn from Laira depot in January 1991. It was bought by the Fifty Fund in November 1991 and entered preservation at St Leonards depot where restoration began. It moved to the SVR in May 1994, where it is based as at December 2016.

50049 entered service as D449 with D05 (Stoke Division) in December 1968 and was withdrawn from Laira depot in August 1991. It was bought by the Class 50 Society in December 1991 and moved to the West Somerset Railway (WSR) in May 1994. Following a period of operation with the Cardiff Valleys Railway Company, it moved to the SVR in 2007, where it is based as at December 2016.

The SVR is the base of operations for the Class 50 Alliance which comprises the three owners of Class 50 locomotives based on the SVR. In 2016, the Alliance established a purpose-built maintenance facility for its diesel locomotives with the secondary purpose of undertaking maintenance work for other diesel locomotive owners. The facility was opened in May 2016 during the SVR's annual diesel gala when three Class 50 locomotives were on display; these were (from left to right) 50049 *Defiance*; 50035 *Ark Royal* and 50044 *Exeter*.

History: This design was in competition with that of the Class 47 for the bulk order of 'standard' locomotives and was essentially the combination of the Deltic (Class 55) bodyshell and the uprated 16-cylinder English Electric engine. The concept had been trialled with prototype locomotive DP2 (Diesel Prototype 2) but BR's CMEE (J.F. 'Freddie' Harrison) demanded a flat-front design which took a lengthy time to complete albeit against the advice of the English Electric design team.

The fleet was initially allocated to the West Coast Main Line (WCML) to operate trains north of Crewe on the non-electrified length north of Weaver Junction but as the electrification extended northwards the released Class 50 locomotives were transferred to the Western Region as replacement for the Class 52 fleet with its hydraulic transmission. The Class 50 fleet was in turn replaced by Multiple Unit and restructured High Speed Train (HST) diagrams but such was the interest in the class that nineteen locomotives entered preservation with some expressly bought for potential main line operation.

During 2009, 50035 *Ark Royal* was renumbered to 50135, to recreate the trialling of classmate 50049 to 50149 by Railfreight that was ultimately reversed, and re-liveried in the Load Haul livery that was lost when English Welsh Scottish Railways (EWSR) took over the freight companies at privatisation. 50035 displays its new embellishments as it approaches Highley on 8 October 2009 with the 15:20 Kidderminster–Highley service during the SVR's annual diesel gala.

50015 entered service as D415 with London Midland Western Lines (LMWL) in April 1968 and was withdrawn from Laira depot in June 1992 from where it was bought by Pete Waterman but quickly transferred to the ownership of the Manchester Class 50 Group. It entered preservation at the East Lancashire Railway (ELR) in October 1992 where it is based as at December 2016.

Right: **50015** *Valiant* **approaches Ramsbottom (ELR) on 4 July 2009 whilst working the 10:06 Rawtenstall–Heywood service during the ELR's annual diesel gala.**

50026 entered service as D426 with D05 (Stoke Division) in July 1968 and was withdrawn from Laira depot in December 1990 whence it was transferred to Booth's scrapyard at Rotherham for scrapping. It was bought from there by a private buyer in April 1993 and, following periods of storage at MOD Bicester and MOD Long Marston, was sent to Railway Vehicle Engineering Ltd (RVEL) at Derby in April 2007 for restoration work. It subsequently moved to the Old Oak Common 'factory' in June 2008 and then to a new base at Eastleigh Works in April 2009 from where the locomotive undertakes main line work and gala visits.

Below: **50026** *Indomitable* **crosses the River Irwell after leaving from Summerseat (ELR) on 5 July 2013 with the 12:05 Heywood–Rawtenstall service during the ELR's annual diesel gala.**

50002 entered service as D402 with London Midland Western Lines (LMWL) in December 1967 and was withdrawn from Laira depot in September 1991. It was bought by the Devon Diesel Society (DDS) and entered preservation at the Paignton & Dartmouth Railway (PDR). It entered an overhaul/operating agreement in 1988 that broke down, leading to legal action and the locomotive returning to the South Devon Railway (SDR) in 2005, where it is based as at December 2016.

Left: During the period of legal action, 50002 *Superb* remained in store at Barrow Hill (BHR) where it was seen on 6 October 2002 during a visit to the site.

50031 entered service as D431 with D05 (Stoke Division) in July 1968 and was withdrawn from Laira depot in August 1991. It was bought by the Fifty Fund and entered preservation at St Leonards depot in March 1992 where restoration began. It gained main line certification and hauled passenger services for both the Cardiff Valleys Railway Company and Arriva Trains Wales before returning to preservation at the Severn Valley Railway (SVR) where it is based as at December 2016.

Right: 50031 *Hood* shows off its Inter City livery at Kidderminster Diesel Depot (SVR) on 21 May 2016 following release by RVEL at Derby after completion of a major overhaul.

50007 entered service as D407 with London Midland Western Lines (LMWL) in March 1968 and was withdrawn from Laira depot in March 1994. It had been painted lined Swindon Green in 1985 and renamed *Sir Edward Elgar* as part of the Western Region's GWR 150 celebrations.

50007 retained its green livery when purchased by the Class 40 Appeal and entered preservation at the Midland Railway Centre (MRC) in July 1994. In October 2013 the locomotive was bought by Boden Rail, reverting to its original livery and name *Hercules*, but subsequently sold on in October 2016 to members of the Class 50 Alliance who moved it to their Kidderminster (SVR) base.

Left: 50007 *Sir Edward Elgar* stands at Oxenhope (KWVR) on 3 August 2002 after arriving with the 13:45 service from Keighley during the KWVR's annual diesel gala.

Opposite: The appeal of the preserved Class 50 fleet is their occasional use on main line duties – especially on enthusiast charters. One such charter ran on 3 August 2002 from Salisbury to Carlisle via the Settle & Carlisle route and is noted powering through Bamber Bridge, shortly after diverging from the WCML, behind 50031 *Hood* and 50049 *Defiance*.

Above: 50044 *Exeter* engages in stock shunting at Highley (SVR) on 8 October 2009 during the SVR's annual diesel gala. The loco is carrying 2-tone green livery which it never bore in BR service but which was applied by its owners to offer a livery variety.

Right: 50044 *Exeter* retains its 2-tone green livery on 2 July 2010 as it curves past Townsend Fold (ELR) at the rear of the 17:06 Rawtenstall–Heywood service during the ELR's annual diesel gala.

2.4.6: Class 52 – BR Workshops

Builder
BR Crewe; BR Swindon

Year Built
1961–1964

Engine
2 x Maybach MD655 rated at 1440 hp @ 1500 rpm built under licence by Bristol-Siddeley

Transmission
Hydraulic

BR Fleet Numbers
D1000–1073; TOPS = Class 52 (TOPS numbers never carried)

History: This design was the Swindon response to the call for a Type 4 design with greater power but continued with the WR 'tradition' of using two engines rather than a single engine as preferred by those advocating electric transmission. Due to delays at Swindon during construction, caused mainly by the WR policy of concentrating repairs at Swindon and undertaking 'unit' replacement at the locomotive depots, construction of D1035–1074 (later supplemented by D1031–1034) was assigned to Crewe Works.

Despite their success and popularity the class was withdrawn in the 1970s following the edict generated from the 1968 National Traction Plan that locomotives with hydraulic transmission were considered as 'non-standard' and therefore to be withdrawn once suitable replacements could be made available.

Right: The Class 52s are popular gala visitors and the East Lancashire Railway (ELR) had two operating during its 2002 annual diesel gala in the shape of the National Rail Museum's (NRM) D1023 *Western Fusilier* and the ELR's resident D1041 *Western Prince*. During a lull in the gala timetable on 6 June 2002 the duo were stabled at Castlecroft depot awaiting their turn of duty.

Opposite: Later in the day the duo were operated in tandem on the 17:10 Bury–Irwell Vale service that ran with Class 45/0 45060 *Sherwood Forester* at the rear as drawback locomotive from Irwell Vale; D1023 *Western Fusilier* pilots D1041 *Western Prince* as they curve across Burrs Common.

D1041 entered service at Old Oak Common depot in June 1962 and was withdrawn from Laira depot in February 1977 whence it was bought by a private individual in May 1977. Following its display at Horwich Works in August 1980 it entered preservation at the East Lancashire Railway (ELR) where it is based as at December 2016.

D1041 *Western Prince* shows its power as it pilots Class 35 'Hymek' D7076 out of Irwell Vale (ELR) on 13 September 2003 whilst working the 13:00 Bury–Rawtenstall service.

D1015 entered service at Cardiff Canton depot in January 1963 and was withdrawn from Laira depot in December 1975 followed by transfer to Swindon Works for display on the works turntable. The locomotive was bought by the Diesel Traction Group (DTG) in January 1980 and restored to, firstly, working order then main line condition to receive main line certification in 2002. The locomotive is a regular gala visitor and operates a small number of main line runs each year. In December 2016 one of the locomotive's two engines failed and the locomotive returned to the Severn Valley Railway (SVR) where it remained as at December 2016, both to operate services with the remaining engine and for DTG members to build the replacement engine funded by the DTG shareholders.

D1015 *Western Champion* undertakes stock shunting at Kidderminster (SVR) on 2 October 2015 prior to working a Kidderminster–Bridgnorth service during the SVR's annual diesel gala.

Left: D1015 *Western Champion* calls at Irwell Vale (ELR) on 4 July 2007 with the 12:05 Heywood–Rawtenstall service during the ELR's annual diesel gala.

D1023 entered service at Cardiff Canton depot in September 1963 and was withdrawn from Laira depot in February 1977 whence it entered preservation at the National Rail Museum (NRM) during 1978.

Right: D1023 *Western Fusilier* climbs past Oakworth Mound (KWVR) on 6 June 2008 whilst approaching Oakworth with the 14:15 Keighley–Oxenhope service during a KWVR diesel gala.

D1062 entered service at Old Oak Common depot in May 1963 and was withdrawn from Laira depot in August 1974. It was bought by the Western Loco Association (WLA) in November 1976 and entered preservation at the Paignton & Dartmouth Railway (PDR) in May 1977; it moved to the Severn Valley Railway (SVR) in August 1978, where it is based at December 2016.

Left: D1062 *Western Courier* eases out of Bewdley (SVR) with the 10:30 Bridgnorth–Kidderminster service on 3 October 2014 during the SVR's annual diesel gala.

2.5: Type 5 Designs

2.5.1: Class 55 – English Electric

Builder
English Electric (Vulcan Foundry)

Year Built
1961–1962

Engine
2 x Napier D18–25 rated at 1650 hp @ 1500 rpm

Transmission
Electric

BR Fleet Numbers
DELTIC; D9000–9021; TOPS = 55001–55022

History: DELTIC was a speculative prototype built by English Electric at its Preston Strand Rd site in October 1955 for which BR's London Midland Region (LMR) provided facilities to trial it between Liverpool and London. The region, however, was more interested in the forthcoming WCML Electrification Project and gave little support to placing orders.

The prototype was subsequently trialled on the ER where the general manager appreciated the possibilities of the design and ordered twenty-two locomotives for use on the ECML services between London and Edinburgh as an interim measure until electrification could be undertaken. In the event they were replaced by High Speed Trainsets (HST) with the final 'Farewell Tour' taking place on 2 January 1982.

DELTIC entered trial service based at Liverpool Speke Junction in October 1955 and was withdrawn from Hornsey depot in March 1961 following serious engine damage. It was stored for a lengthy period until donated to the Science Museum in 1963 and a subsequent move to the National Rail Museum (NRM) at York in 1993. It was loaned to the Ribble Steam Railway (RSR) between August 2012 and October 2015 to commemorate the fact that the RSR line passes close to the site where DELTIC was built.

To celebrate its 60th birthday DELTIC was posed at Preston Strand Road Crossing on 14 September 2015 at a point where the locomotive would have joined the BR network after being released from the Dick Kerr/English Electric factory – a site operated by Alstom as at December 2016.

Preservation History: After withdrawal from service during December 1981 and January 1982, the surviving class members were moved to Doncaster Works for scrapping. A 'Farewell Line-Up' was held on 27 February 1982 from which six class members managed to enter preservation. These suffered diverse fates but as at December 2016 there are two owning groups for these survivors with the Deltic Preservation Society (DPS) owning three locomotives (D9009/9015/9019) and Beaver Sports owning two locomotives (D9000/9016) whilst D9002 is part of the National Rail Museum collection.

D9000/55022 entered service at Haymarket depot in February 1961 and was withdrawn from York depot in January 1982, whence it was sold to the Deltic9000 Fund which returned the locomotive to main line service. On the demise of the company in 2004 the locomotive was bought by Beaver Sports and entered preservation at Barrow Hill Roundhouse (BHR) in December 2004. The locomotive subsequently moved to the East Lancashire Railway (ELR) but moved to the North Yorkshire Moors in April 2016 following completion of main line work. Although nominally 'preserved' D9000 retains full main line certification and, since ownership by Beaver Sports, is effectively a 'spot hire' locomotive although based on heritage lines between hire contracts.

D9002/55002 entered service at Gateshead depot in March 1961 and was withdrawn from York depot in January 1982. Initially reserved for the last train in January 1982, engine failure saw it being withdrawn and transferred to the NRM.

D9009/55009 entered service at Finsbury Park depot in January 1961 and was withdrawn from York depot in January 1982. It was bought by the DPS and entered preservation with the North Yorkshire Moors Railway (NYMR) in August 1982, subsequently moving to Barrow Hill (BHR) in December 1998 where the locomotive is based as at December 2016.

D9015/55015 entered service at Finsbury Park depot in October 1961 and was withdrawn from York depot in December 1981. Unusually offered for sale by auction in 1982 it failed to sell but was bought by a private buyer in 1984 and entered preservation at the Midland Railway Centre (MRC) in February 1984. It was bought by the DPS in 1986 and moved to the new DPS base at Barrow Hill (BHR) in September 2003 for a full overhaul.

D9016/55016 entered service at Haymarket depot in October 1961 and was withdrawn from York depot in December 1981. It was bought by Deltic9000 Fund as spares for D9000. On the company's demise in 2004 the locomotive passed through various ownerships until bought by Beaver Sports in December 2009 and effectively entered preservation at the East Lancashire Railway (ELR). The locomotive moved to a new base at the Great Central Railway (GCR) in 2014 but as at December 2016 it is undergoing a full restoration at the Boden Rail workshops at Washwood Heath.

D9019/55019 entered service at Haymarket depot in December 1961 and was withdrawn from York depot in December 1981. It was sold to the DPS and entered preservation at the NYMR with D9009/55009. It subsequently gained main line certification and became the flagship locomotive for the DPS as the latter established its base at Barrow Hill (BHR) where it opened its dedicated maintenance facility on 20 September 2003.

Left: The new DPS depot was opened to the public on 5 October 2003 when D9009 *Alycidon*, D9015 *Tulyar* and 55019 *Royal Highland Fusilier* were on display.

Right: The DPS celebrated Doncaster's 'Farewell Line-Up' of February 1981 on 12 August 2006 with all six surviving locomotives on display. At the end of the day D9015 *Tulyar* and D9009 *Alycidon* await their return to the depot.

The ELR celebrated the 50th anniversary of the class's introduction to service by hosting all five working preserved locomotives during a gala weekend in which the highlight on 15 October 2011 was the Saturday 'BEEREX' powered by all five locomotives. The convoy passed Ramsbottom on the Bury–Rawtenstall leg behind 55022 *Royal Scots Grey* + 55019 *Royal Highland Fusilier* + 55002 *Kings Own Yorkshire Light Infantry* + D9009 *Alycidon* + D9016 *Gordon Highlander*. D9016 was working on one engine hence the available horsepower of the combination was a massive 4 x 3300 hp + 1650 hp = 14850 HP!

On 12 August 2006 the DPS held a gala event at its Barrow Hill base to commemorate the end of Deltic-hauled services in 1981 and recall the Doncaster line-up of the withdrawn locomotives in February 1982 under the banner of the 'Doncaster Tribute' at which all six preserved locomotives were in attendance.

Top Left: In the 'blue corner' posed 55022 *Royal Scots Grey*; 55002 *Kings Own Yorkshire Light Infantry* and 55019 *Royal Highland Fusilier*.

Top Right: In the (2-tone) 'green corner' posed D9016 *Gordon Highlander*; D9009 *Alycidon* and D9015 *Tulyar*.

Left: In the yard, all six came together.

Right: D9009 *Alycidon* pilots failed Class 40 D335 past Townsend Fold (ELR) on 5 July 2014 whilst working the delayed 13:55 Heywood–Rawtenstall service during the ELR's annual diesel gala.

Left: 55022 *Royal Scots Grey* works in top 'n tail mode with 55019 *Royal Highland Fusilier* on 12 August 2006 whilst working the Barrow Hill (BHR) shuttle service.

Right: 55022 *Royal Scots Grey* is pilotted by D9016 *Gordon Highlander* as they work in top 'n tail mode with Class 37/4 37418 *Pectinidae* to cross Burrs Common (ELR) with the 15:20 Heywood–Rawtenstall service on 9 January 2010.

2.5.2: *Class 56 – Brush Traction*

Builder
Brush Traction; BR Crewe; BR Doncaster

Year Built
1976–1984

Engine
Ruston Paxman 16RK3CT rated at 3250 hp @ 900 rpm

Transmission
Electric

BR Fleet Numbers
56001–56135

History: This class was part of a 'technology transfer' in which Brush Traction built the component parts of 56001–56030 and exported them to Romania for assembly but, when the completed locomotives were returned from August 1976, major problems were found, necessitating corrective action before they could enter service.

56031–135 were subsequently ordered from Doncaster Works but when the Class 56 was redesigned as the Class 58, construction of 56116–135 was transferred to Crewe Works. Notable for being the first diesel class to carry TOPS fleet numbers from new, many were withdrawn from service by English Welsh Scottish Railways (EWSR) when Class 66 deliveries began from 1998 but some survived into preservation, some were hired to French infrastructure companies and some survived to be bought by new train operating companies.

56003 arrived from Romania in August 1976 but only entered service at Tinsley depot in February 1977 and was withdrawn from Immingham depot in April 1999 whence it was sent to Booth's scrapyard for disposal. It was bought privately and transferred to Long Marston where it was restored to operational condition and made its first appearance in preservation at the Gloucester Warwickshire Railway (GWR) in July 2005. It was subsequently bought by Hanson Traction in 2008 and returned to main line operation as 56312. As at December 2016 it is operated by British American Rail Services (BARS) which bought Hanson Traction in 2010.

Below Left: 56003 carries LoadHaul livery as it enters Ramsbottom (ELR) on 7 July 2006 with the 11:05 Rawtenstall–Heywood service during the ELR's annual diesel gala.

56057 entered service at Toton depot in March 1979 and was withdrawn from Immingham depot in July 1999 from where it was bought by Neil Boden in 2004 and entered preservation at the Nene Valley Railway (NVR). The locomotive was subsequently bought by Hanson Traction in 2006 and renumbered 56311 when returned to main line service.

Below Right: Neil Boden works on his recently bought 56057 at Wansford (NVR) on 14 August 2004.

2.5.3: Class 58 – BR Workshops

Builder
BR Doncaster

Year Built
1983–1987

Engine
Ruston Paxman 12RK3CT rated at 3300 hp @ 1000 rpm

Transmission
Electric

BR Fleet Numbers
58001–58050

History: This class was a development of the Class 56 design which included easier engine access to support possible export sales that never arose and the fleet was based at Toton depot to power coal traffic services in the East Midlands. When BR was privatised the fleet was an early candidate for withdrawal but many class members were retained for hire to French and Spanish infrastructure companies to assist with their high speed rail construction projects.

58016 entered service at Toton depot in October 1984 and was withdrawn from Eastleigh depot in August 2002 and transferred to the 'hire' fleet. It was hired to Fertis for use in France between May 2005 and May 2006 then withdrawn from service and placed into store. It was bought by the Class 58 Locomotive Group (C58LG) and entered preservation at Barrow Hill (BHR) in June 2010 where restoration to working order began. The locomotive moved to the Leicester base of UK Rail Leasings (UKRL) in 2016 where its restoration continues as at December 2016.

Above: Work underway at Barrow Hill (BHR) on 29 September 2013.

Below: Work underway at Barrow Hill (BHR) on 6 February 2014.

Section 3:
Heritage Centres

The preserved diesel locomotives are operated by many heritage lines, both as standby traction in cases of steam locomotive failures or for speedy availability to assist with the mundane tasks involved in infrastructure maintenance. Some of the larger heritage lines make a virtue of their diesel fleet by regularly operating them on timetabled services whilst some go further and operate gala events dedicated to this type of traction.

Many of these centres have been noted in the images for specific locomotive classes but this has not shown the variety of locomotives that are brought together for gala events and this is made good in this section. One aspect of the modern heritage scene is the willingness of locomotive owners to display their locomotives at distant sites and this section is dedicated to both the heritage lines hosting the event(s) and the locomotive owners willing to take the time and make the effort to support them.

3.1: Barrow Hill Roundhouse (BHR)

Barrow Hill Roundhouse (BHR) opened in 1998 to preserve the last operational roundhouse shed in the UK with a history going back to the opening of the depot by the Midland Railway (MR) in 1870. Its initial aim was to preserve the facility by offering facilities for the restoration of preserved locomotives but that quickly outstripped resources especially when railway engineering and preservation groups established themselves on site. One of the largest firms is Harry Needle Railway Company (HNRC) whose business of locomotive maintenance/hire has expanded since moving onto site and who generously supports preservation by providing locomotives to gala events throughout the country whilst denying that he is a preservationist.

The site operates a number of galas each operating season, although not confined to just diesel traction, and opens at various times throughout the year.

An interior of the roundhouse as seen on 21 October 2006 with diesel and electric locomotives shrouded in smoke from steam locomotives positioned around the turntable behind the photographer. In this image are (from left to right) Class 07 07012; Class 81 81002; Class 56 56006; Class 25/1 25067; Class 26 26011 and Class 33/1 33111.

Further information on this heritage centre is available at www.barrowhill.org

Left: During gala events at Barrow Hill the storage yard of HNRC is used to stable locomotives from the roundhouse to provide extra space for the gala displays and events. On 6 February 2014 the stabled locomotives included (from left to right) Class 56 56006; Class 86/2 86213 *Lancashire Witch*; Class 84 84001; A selection of Class 20s; Class 40 D212 *Aureol* and Class 71 E5001.

Right: A view of the roundhouse interior on 29 September 2013 shows preserved locomotives around the turntable in various stages of restoration including Class 58 58016; Class 45/0 45060 *Sherwood Forester*; Class 37 37057; Class 26 doyen 26007 (D5300); Class 83 83012 and Class 81 81002.

Left: A collection of preserved diesel locomotives, stored in the HNRC yard during a Barrow Hill Steam Gala on 12 July 2003, includes Class 55 'Deltic' 55019 *Royal Highland Fusilier* and D9009 *Alycidon*; Class 45/0 45060 *Sherwood Forester* and Class 26 26011.

3.2: Bo'ness & Kinneil Railway (BKR)

The Scottish Railway Preservation Society (SRPS) was established in 1961 to preserve railway artefacts peculiar to the various Scottish Railway companies which both built and operated railways and rolling stock within Scotland. On 1964 it found a site in Falkirk where it began to accumulate and display its collection but in 1979 elected to move to a bigger non-railway site in nearby Bo'ness. By 1981 it was able to run shuttle services in its new station area which it extended to Kinneil (a mile from Bo'ness) in 1981. Further progress was slow with service extensions to Birkhill (4.5 miles from Bo'ness) by 1989.

In 1987 the SRPS had to leave the Falkirk site due to redevelopment schemes and hence had to lay a 1.5-mile rail connection from Birkhill to Manuel to connect with the Edinburgh–Glasgow Queen St main line in order to transfer the rolling stock to Bo'ness. In 2010 this line was upgraded for passenger use and the service is now operated from Bo'ness to Manuel.

Adjacent to the station at Bo'ness the SRPS has established the Scottish Railway Museum where it exhibits its many artefacts – including locomotives awaiting overhaul.

Further information on this heritage centre is available at www.bkrailway.co.uk

The SRPS locomotive collection includes diesel locomotives that have operated rail services within Scotland and a visit to Bo'ness on 23 February 2009 captured the scene of a line-up that included (from left to right) Class 27 doyen 27001; Class 26 26024; Class 37/4 37413; Class 26 D5310; North British 0-4-0 Shunter D2767; Class 20 D8020 and Class 25/2 25235 (D7585).

3.3: *Embsay & Bolton Abbey Railway (EBAR)*

The Yorkshire Dales Railway Society (YDRS) was formed in 1968 to preserve the Midland Railway (MR) line between Skipton and Ilkley that had been closed in 1965 and established its initial base at Embsay on the outskirts of Skipton. This opened in 1979 with a shuttle service being introduced in 1981. The junction with the Skipton–Swinden Quarry/Grassington Branch was cut in 1982 leading the YDR to prioritise reopening the line towards Bolton Abbey and Ilkley with a secondary aim of re-establishing the connection to Skipton.

Progress was slow with openings at Holywell Halt in 1987, Stoneacre Loop in 1991 and finally at Bolton Abbey in 1998 after which the YDR transformed into the Embsay & Bolton Abbey Railway (EBAR).

Since the reopening of Bolton Abbey, consideration has been given to reopening the line to Addingham then Ilkley, but developments on the trackbed since closure have made this an expensive option whilst the continuing discussions to reconnect the line to the Grassington Branch have been met with little support from Network Rail.

Further information on this heritage centre is available at www.embsaybolton abbeyrailway.org.uk

Left: A station scene at Embsay on 25 July 2010 as Class 31 D5600/31435 stands in the platform, Class 14 D9513 (in its industrial guise as NCB 38) awaits departure with a service to Bolton Abbey, and Class 04 D2203 shunts stock in the depot yard.

Below: Class 08 08773/D3941 stands at Embsay platform on 25 March 2006 as Class 04 D2203 arrives from the truncated Bow Lane with a shuttle service.

Opposite Page: A 1960s scene recreated during a weekend diesel gala on 29 October 2006 sees Class 20 20189/D8189 stabled at Bolton Abbey after failing whilst a Class 107 2-car trainset undergoes attention and Class 47/0 D1524 awaits departure with a Bolton Abbey–Embsay service.

119

3.4: East Lancashire Railway (ELR)

The beginnings of the East Lancashire Railway (ELR) arose at Helmshore in 1966 when a scheme was initiated to restore services to the Helmshore–Accrington section of the Ramsbottom–Helmshore–Accrington line which was being closed as one of the Beeching closures. Despite local support there was insufficient funding to prevent BR lifting the line in October 1971 and the ELR was forced to look elsewhere. That 'elsewhere' was Castlecroft Goods Warehouse, then in use by contractors building a local bypass; once vacated it was then leased by Bury Metropolitan Council (BMC) to the ELR and stock was transferred during May 1972 from Helmshore.

The main thrust of future growth came from the desire of local councils to develop the Irwell Valley which was initiated in 1981 when ELR representatives met with local councils to explain how a railway could provide the boost by acting as a catalyst. The councils responded by buying the trackbed from Bury to Rawtenstall then leasing it to the nascent ELR. Progress was sufficiently rapid that following the lease being granted, train services to Ramsbottom restarted in July 1987 and to Rawtenstall in

November 1989. Encouraged by this development Rochdale Council supported an easterly extension to Heywood which opened in September 2003.

The Bury–Heywood line became important after redevelopment of the Bury Metrolink had closed off the original access to the BR network at Bury; the new link provided via Heywood at Castleton made easier the transfer of rolling stock between the two systems. Whilst the link was available from February 1994, when it was used for the first time by Class 8 4-6-2 71000 *Duke of Gloucester*, it was September 2003 before the first Bury–Heywood passenger service began.

Each July the ELR operates a diesel gala which operates both home-based locomotives and a variety of locomotives visiting from other heritage centres. This event now attracts a large number of visitors and is second only to the Father Christmas season of trains as a major stream of income.

Further information on this heritage centre is available at www.eastlancsrailway.org.uk

A scene from the 2003 gala on 5 July sees Class 52 D1041 *Western Prince* bring the shuttle stock from the sidings into the station prior to working a Ramsbottom–Bury service that had been brought in by Class 45/0 45060 *Sherwood Forester* whilst Class 31 D5600/31435 is stabled on 'Thunderbird' duty.

A scene from the 2006 gala on 7 July sees Class 56 56003 (in LoadHaul livery) passing Castlecroft depot with a Bury–Rawtenstall service whilst Class 45/1 45135 *3rd Carabinier*, Class 26 26024 and Class 47/4 47402 *Gateshead* await their next duties.

3.5: Great Central Railway (GCR)

The Great Central Railway (GCR) ran from Manchester via Sheffield, Nottingham, Leicester and Rugby to London Marylebone but was closed in stages until the final section between Rugby and Nottingham closed in 1969. A group of enthusiasts formed the Main Line Preservation Group (MNPG) with the aim of reopening the line for use by main line steam locomotives but fund-raising proved difficult and the Main Line Steam Trust (MLST) was formed in 1971 to continue fund-raising.

This proved equally unsuccessful and in 1976 the Great Central Railway (1976) was formed. This managed to buy the Loughborough–Rothley single track section but, supported by the local council which bought the Loughborough Central–Birstall trackbed, the small single track line has grown in stages to provide a double track main line between Loughborough Central and Leicester North, just south of Birstall.

Further information on this heritage centre is available at www.gcrailway.co.uk

The GCR suffers from a shortage of siding space hence its diesel locomotives are stabled in a dedicated siding at Loughborough Central station, the base of the GCR's operations.

The line-up during a visit on 15 August 2005 was led by Class 31/1 D5830 and included Class 47 D1705 *Sparrow Hawk*; Class 20 D8048; Class 73/0 E6003 *Sir Herbert Walker* KCB and Class 25/1 D5185.

The line-up during a visit on 13 November 2008 was led by Class 27 D5401 and included Class 25/1 D5185; Class 47 D1705 *Sparrow Hawk*; Class 37/3 37314 *Dalzell* and Class 31/1 D5830.

3.6: Keighley & Worth Valley Railway (KWVR)

The Worth Valley branch line was closed in 1962 and local support saw the creation of the Keighley & Worth Valley Railway Preservation Society (KWVRPS) with the aim of buying the branch line from Keighley to Oxenhope in order to operate a local service. The line was bought from BR, the first such sale ever made by BR, and the KWVRPS began to restore the line whilst seeking locomotives and rolling stock to provide a service. Success came in 1968 when the first Keighley–Oxenhope services began using locomotives based at Haworth where the base of the line has been established.

Further information on this heritage centre is available at www.kwvr.co.uk

The beginning of each day during the KWVR gala events is marked by the preparation of all the locomotives in Haworth shed yard resulting in the line-up of participating locomotives.

Top Right: **The line-up on 25 May 2012 for the 2012 diesel gala includes (from left to right) Class 108 DMU 51565; Class 33/1 33103 *Swordfish*; Class 31/4 31466; Class 37 37075; Class 50 50026 *Indomitable* and shed pilot Class 08 08266.**

Bottom Right: **The line-up on 27 April 2013 for the 2013 diesel gala includes (from left to right) Class 101 DMU 51803; Class 26 26038; Class 20 20020; Class 25/3 D7628 *Sybilla*; Class 25/1 25059; shed pilot resident Class 08 08266 and Class 20 20031.**

Opposite Page: **A dreary day at Oxenhope on 15 June 2007 during the 2007 diesel gala sees Class 20 visitor D8020 + resident 20031 depart with the 12:45 Oxenhope–Keighley service whilst Class 25/1 25059 waits in the carriage siding for its next duty.**

3.7: Severn Valley Railway (SVR)

The Severn Valley line from Kidderminster to Bridgnorth closed to passengers in 1963 and in June 1965 the Severn Valley Railway Society (SVRS) was formed to buy the line from Bridgnorth to Alveley Colliery where freight traffic still operated. When this traffic ceased, efforts began to buy further land resulting in Sir Gerald Nabarro, the local MP, heading a share campaign that successfully raised £74,000 to buy the line from Alveley Colliery to Foley Park with services extending in stages to Bewdley during 1974. In 1982 the British Sugar Corporation closed its Kidderminster site resulting in the SVR buying the remaining 1.5-mile trackbed into Kidderminster where a new terminus was built. This was opened in 1984 and the SVR has continued developing its facilities/line/services between Kidderminster and Bridgnorth.

Further information on this heritage centre is available at www.svr.co.uk

The SVR diesel galas normally occur in October, once the annual Autumn Steam Gala has been held, and mark the end of the operating season after which preparations begin for the Santa Specials that operate during December each year.

In 2014 the gala was dedicated to English Electric locomotives and on 3 October the early morning scene at Kidderminster saw (from left to right) Class 40 40106 *Atlantic Conveyor* waiting to shunt the stock of a Kidderminster–Bridgnorth service; class 37/0 37109 awaiting departure for Bridgnorth and Class 55 'Deltic' 55019 *Royal Highland Fusilier* awaiting its next duty.

In the purpose-built terminus at Kidderminster the epitome of the Western Region was created on 2 October 2015 with Class 52 'Western' D1015 *Western Champion* preparing to shunt stock for a Kidderminster–Bridgnorth service; Class 35 'Hymek' D7029 stabled behind as a display item; Class 14 D9531 awaiting departure on a Kidderminster–Bewdley shuttle service and Class 50 'Hoover' 50049 *Defiance* stabled at the platform as a display item.

Shortly before the previous image was taken, the scene reflected the later Changeover Years as D1015 *Western Champion* was posed alongside Class 50 'Hoover' 50035 *Ark Royal* awaiting departure on a Kidderminster–Bridgnorth service.

The SVR and the various locomotive owners have invested in the future of their diesel fleet by building a purpose-built maintenance depot at Kidderminster which was officially opened on 20 May 2016 during the annual diesel gala. Open to the public during the 3-day event, a visit on 21 May revealed a display of Class 50 'Hoover' 50035 *Ark Royal*, Class 35 'Hymek' D7029 and Class 52 'Western' D1062 *Western Courier* settling into their new base.